The Action to the Word

The Action to the Word

Structure and Style in Shakespearean Tragedy

David Young

Yale University Press
New Haven and London

Published with assistance from the Kingsley Trust Association Publication Fund established by the Scroll and Key Society of Yale College.

Designed by Nancy Ovedovitz and set in Fournier type by Brevis Press, Bethany, Connecticut. Printed in the United States of America.

Library of Congress Cataloging-in-Publication Data

Young, David, 1936–
The action to the word : structure and style in Shakespearean tragedy / David Young.
    p. cm.   Bibliography: p.
    Includes index.
    ISBN 0–300–04534–4 (alk. paper)
    1. Shakespeare, William, 1564–1616—Tragedies.   I. Title.
PR2983.Y6   1990
822.3'3—dc20   89–33132
                                                              CIP

The paper in this book meets the guidelines for permanence and durability of the Committee on Production Guidelines for Book Longevity of the Council on Library Resources.

10   9   8   7   6   5   4   3   2   1

for Maynard Mack

Contents

Preface

The temptation to enlarge this study, especially so as to include *Coriolanus* and *Antony and Cleopatra*, is one that I was finally able to resist. To treat four plays and treat them well seemed a sufficient challenge, indeed an awesome one. So much has been written about these plays that one cannot help wondering whether anything further need be said. The question is a healthy one, and so is its companion query: how much here is really new? I hope, of course, that there is enough fresh insight in these chapters to entertain and enlighten even those who have climbed for years among the mountains of Shakespearean commentary. I have tried to write for them, as well as for readers who have less familiarity with Shakespeare and his vast army of interpreters. Along the way I have been encouraged by the thought that clear, straightforward writing—an ideal I subscribe to, even if I may not always achieve it—has usually served Shakespeare and his readers best. In other words, I too have tried to suit the action to the word, the word to the action. It is probably folly for a critic to protest, as Polonius does to Gertrude, that he or she uses no art at all, but trying not to overstep the modesty of nature remains an attractive, if unspectacular, ideal. In any case, readers should understand that my resistance to contemporary fashions in criticism, including the penchant for jargon, is deliberate rather than naive.

A word is in order about editions. After some pondering about the multiple choices open to me, I have decided to take my citations of the texts of the tragedies discussed in this book from the Arden editions of the plays, published by Methuen. These are widely available and, for the most part, superbly edited. The possible exception is M. R. Ridley's edition of *Othello,* which cultivates what many people feel is an eccentric preference for the Quarto text. Having made the Arden commitment, however, I have held to it except where otherwise noted. I wish to add, though, that it has been a great help to me to have at hand the New Variorum editions of the plays—edited by H. H. Furness a century ago and still full of interesting information and sensible presentation—and the Norton facsimile of the First Folio, prepared by Charlton Hinman (New York, 1987). Where textual issues have taken me beyond the Arden editions, I have noted my sources and the issues they raise in separate footnotes.

Parts of this book were first tried out in various settings over the past ten years. Papers on several different aspects of *Macbeth,* given at the State University of New York at Rochester and at Wells College in 1978, and at the 1979 MLA and the 1980 NCTE conventions, came first. Two papers on *Othello* were next—one given as the keynote address at the 1981 meeting of the Shakespeare and Renaissance Association of West Virginia, the other read in November 1981, while I was enjoying a fellowship at the Huntington Library, at a symposium entitled "Shakespeare's Renaissance," jointly sponsored by USC, UCLA, and the Clark Library. A paper on *Hamlet* was given first at a Yale symposium in honor of Maynard Mack in April 1984 and then, in a revised version, as the inaugural lecture for the Longman Chair in English and Humanities at Oberlin College in 1986. A course I offered on Shakespearean tragedy at the Breadloaf School of English in the summer of 1983 helped considerably in shaping my ideas about the book. So did a kind of ongoing dialogue with my own students and colleagues at Oberlin, always a lively place to study and think about Shakespeare. Oberlin's other significant contribution was a Research Status Appointment for 1987–88, which allowed me to complete the writing of the book.

Thanks are always inadequate in such a circumstance as this. How to acknowledge coherently all the previous commentators on Shakespeare who have helped, whether through agreement or through disagreement with one's own views, to clarify the plays? How to document valuable suggestions made in dialogue at conferences and discussions with colleagues, or in the give-and-take of teaching? The book is more lightly annotated than some will wish. The dilemma has been to know what deserves including. Should I, for example, since my interest in performance is a substantial factor in my critical approach, mention the recent body of critical literature that takes up that perspective, such as David Bevington's excellent *Action Is Eloquence?* Or should I, since my inspiration predates that literature and stems from years of theater-going and from acting in amateur productions, refrain from misleading readers about my sources? My tendency has been to be sparing about citation. I have not cited Bevington, whose book I came to after this one was virtually complete. Neither have I cited productions in which I got to play Falstaff, the King in *All's Well That Ends Well,* or Toby Belch. Nor was there any way I could cite all the classroom sessions that helped produce many of the best insights in this book.

The few must stand for the many. I have two citations to students who were in the Breadloaf course. They must represent not only their classmates but also the Oberlin undergraduates whom I have taught over many years. Similarly, the people I name now, who have been especially helpful as readers and commentators on this manuscript, must also symbolize many others who have contributed ideas and reactions in more fragmentary ways.

Phyllis Gorfain, my colleague at Oberlin, read the chapters in draft and made many helpful suggestions. Maynard Mack and William C. Carroll, the one a mentor and constant example for scholarship and criticism, the other a former student turned compeer and compatriot, read the draft of the whole and helped me refine my ideas, clarify my prose, and back away from some of my more foolish assertions. The anonymous reader for Yale University Press contributed many valuable suggestions, as did Ellen Graham, my editor, and Cynthia Wells, senior production editor at the Press, went over the manuscript with prodigious care and wonderful sensitivity. Georgia Newman, wife and mate, brought patience, love, and support in unstinting amounts, especially during the year in which I was engaged in writing and assembling the book's final version.

The Action to the Word

Introduction

When I began this study of Shakespeare's tragedies, the question I wished to pose was why they differed so markedly from each other. The playwright's restlessness, his urge to explore the limits of a genre, was the one common ground I could discern among his four most admired tragedies. Their experimental tendency might, I felt, be the only characteristic they shared, in which case my efforts at seeing them as a group could have a precarious unity at best.

As I worked on, however, a common feature began to emerge among the plays I was treating. Each of them had some kind of profound and productive tension between dramatic action and expressive language. By acknowledging and exploiting conflicts between the action of a play and its characteristic uses of language, Shakespeare, I discovered, was able to confront problems the solutions of which contributed significantly to the distinctiveness and richness of his tragedies. He need not have been particularly conscious of this habit to have made repeated and even deliberate use of it. Instinctive creative choices by an author who happened to be both a gifted poet and a working man of the theater, a sort of actor-manager, could well account for the pattern I saw emerging.

But it is not simply a matter of Shakespeare's personality and interests. The tension between action and language, movement and speech, gesture and word, may well be endemic to theater, which has always before it the twin extremes of pantomime and closet drama—a theater without words on the one hand and, on the other, a theater so dominated by language that it is more effective for reading and listening than for physical performance. To put it another way: all plays seem to spring from a dual urge to portray conflict and the actions that result from it and to comment expressively on that conflict. By means of soliloquies, set pieces, choric commentaries, and other such devices, playwrights raise language from the relatively straightforward function of dialogue to a more reflexive and contemplative condition, one that aspires to all the resources of expression and meaning of which human speech is capable.

The interdependence of these elements in great drama does not mean that there is no conflict between them. It rather suggests that the playwright has brought their separate urges for hegemony into an uneasy but productive truce. Plot, we might say, aspires to be all action and movement, while language aspires to have nothing but its "say," to comment endlessly and eloquently on what is happening and what it means. Insofar as these selfish urges are thwarted, drama, always a collaborative art, comes into its own.

Certainly the tension I am describing was a factor in the Renaissance and on the Elizabethan stage. If we ask why in Shakespeare's time drama was more successful and vigorous in England than it was in Italy, where other arts like painting, music, architecture, and sculpture flourished, one answer has to be that Italian drama was divided between plays with literary aspirations and plays with popular theatrical energies. We would not want to be without either of the traditions that produced the *commedia dell'arte* on the one hand and plays like Guarini's *Il pastor fido* and Tasso's *Aminta* on the other, but it is when we imagine the fusing of such traditions that we begin to understand the theater that produced not only Shakespeare but Marlowe, Jonson, Webster, and Middleton, as well. The vigorous and enchanting playing of the popular actors of the

Italian stage is now a matter of hearsay and speculation, since the plots they used were only outlines from which they improvised. The literary excellence of the *erudita* plays has been preserved at the cost of real performance interest. We have their texts to perform, but no great urge to stage them, whereas the texts of Shakespeare and his contemporaries still demand theatrical realization if we are to understand and evaluate them fully.

English playwrights did not achieve their balanced command of vigorous action and eloquent language without a struggle. In the playwrights who preceded Shakespeare and in his own early work, we see resolutions being worked out, not always very successfully, to the vexing problem of when to move and when to speak, when to propel the action and when to comment on its meaning. To be stageworthy and poetic at the same time was no easy matter, and sometimes playwrights succeeded in being neither. Still, the matter was attacked with enthusiasm and dedication by such figures as Peele, Greene, Lyly, Marlowe, and Kyd. In Kyd's *Spanish Tragedy* there is often a kind of seesaw effect, as violent action grinds to a halt in order to make room for outbursts of rhetorical language based on the model of Seneca, whose poetic dramas showed little concern for performability. Kyd's play achieved enormous popularity by simply pouring on the effects in both departments, as if to make up for their lack of integration. We notice its problems partly because the rhetoric is finally not very successful.[1]

When we come to Marlowe's two *Tamburlaine* plays, on the other hand, we may overlook relative weaknesses of plot and structure because the poetry *is* so successful. In its sweep and vitality the language embodies energies we would normally expect to see expressed through stage action. We could say that both Kyd and early Marlowe are rather operatic, with the difference that Marlowe writes much more enchanting arias. Both are in the literary vein, and their great popularity comes despite their deficiencies in dramaturgy. Marlowe, however, for all the brevity of his career, obviously was busy teaching himself to modulate the poetic expressiveness of *Tamburlaine I* and *II* and *Doctor Faustus* in favor of plays that balance verbal eloquence and stage action. *The Jew of Malta* and *Edward II* are almost too crammed with activity, as if to compensate for the playwright's own gifts and propensities. How Marlowe might have continued remains a matter of pure conjecture. His momentum was in effect taken over by his most thoughtful imitator and rival, William Shakespeare.

Shakespeare's own beginnings reflect the same awkwardness at integrating eloquent language with effective action that afflicted his contemporaries. Perhaps the most famous example among his early plays is that moment in *Titus Andronicus* when Marcus encounters Lavinia, his niece, who has just been raped and had her hands and tongue cut off. Dramatic action, the logic of which demands that he comfort her and get her some medical attention, grinds to a halt—or a near-halt; some actions by Lavinia, such as turning away, are implied by what Marcus says—while Marcus delivers a speech of forty-seven lines, filled with classical analogies (to Tereus, Philomel, Titan, Cerberus, Orpheus) and with tropes (arms as branches, blood as a river, grief as a sealed oven, hands as aspen leaves, tears as a flood) that are more likely to produce impatience than delight. Following the track of Senecan rhetoric has put the young playwright in conflict with his own instinct to make language and action work together.

After *Titus Andronicus* (I will limit myself here to a consideration of the tragedies and histories), Shakespeare progresses rapidly in his exploration of the potential for balance between expressive language and engrossing action. The historical tetralogy that culminates in *Richard III* is full of interesting experiments and clumsy transitions and devices. By comparison with later Shakespeare, the rhetorical commitments in these plays make them cumbersome, but they are exciting and operatic in the same way that Marlowe and Kyd are; instead of being discouraged by the challenge of combining poetry with stage action, the youthful playwright is clearly stimulated and invigorated by it.

Shakespeare's first great solution to the problem of balancing eloquent language and vigorous action comes in the somewhat stylized form we find in early masterpieces like *Richard II* and *Romeo and Juliet*. These plays have a confidence and energy that is quite breathtaking. We assign them to a "formal" period because both their language and their action require a certain amount of stylization—emphasis on ritual and form, extensive parallelism and rhyme—to achieve harmonious integration. If it had happened that Shakespeare's career, like Marlowe's, had been suddenly cut off, say at 1595, we would certainly know him as a great playwright who resolved the dramaturgical problems faced by his contemporaries.

But of course he went on. And as he did so, he continued to address the question of balancing speech and action, in play after play, with an increasing ease and fascination. One result of his continued experimentation is a greater naturalism, in the *Henry* plays and in *Julius Caesar*. Both the poetry and the action are less stylized and ritualized than had previously been the case. Characters like Falstaff and eloquence of the kind we find in Cassius are difficult to imagine in earlier plays, although Mercutio and the Nurse in *Romeo and Juliet* certainly foreshadow the more naturalistic handling of speech and action in the middle and late plays. In any case, we can observe that by the time Shakespeare was working on *Hamlet*, he was ready to challenge himself in ways that Marlowe and Kyd (who had probably written the earlier Hamlet play) never dreamed of. The results are well known, but they have never been consistently and fully addressed from the perspective I propose to pursue in this study.

My terminology has thus far been a little slippery. I see this as an acceptable necessity. None of the paired terms we might resort to for the tension I claim Shakespeare was exploring and exploiting—speech and action, poetry and plot, word and deed, style and structure—quite succeed in summarizing or defining the nature of this opposition. Its presence is not difficult to recognize, for instance, when Hamlet talks about good acting as suiting "the action to the word, the word to the action," or when Macbeth characterizes life as a poor player who "struts and frets his hour upon the stage." Recognizing its presence is one thing; giving it definitive names is another.

I could solve this problem superficially by finding a couple of fierce Greek words; classical terms, especially from the Greek, always seem to give the impression that a critic has licked the problem of successful definition. The speech-action opposition, however, belongs to an artistic medium that is too mercurial and dynamic to be fixed by easy terminology. Thus I think it better to try to surround my oppositions by a series of suggestions: by noting, for example, that we acknowledge them when we say a play is too "talky" (as is said of Shaw or Giraudoux); by observing that they are related to the visual and aural dimensions of performance, so that spectacle and music are among their possibilities and representatives; and by admitting that a book with a different aim than this one might well devote lengthy chapters to an exploration of drama's divided impulse to strut and to fret.

If the pair of terms that surfaces most often in my discussion is the pair of the subtitle, *style* and *structure,* that is because those terms refer implicitly to conscious artistry and thus to our sense that the successful playwright should hope to accomplish a distinctive use of language as well as a comely shaping of events. No doubt verbal style is finally a part of structure in the fullest sense of that word, while the design of the dramatic action of a play involves, or ought to involve, the eloquent and expressive use of language (unless the aim is pantomime). But *style* and *structure* imply emphasis, one on language and the other on action, even if they don't achieve purity, and emphasis is what the capacious, fluent world of performance is all about.

One other difficulty that needs to be raised at the outset: I speak at many points of a "tension" between structure and style, action and word, strut and fret. Is this a tension Shakespeare introduces to his plays, or one that he found there waiting for him? I would say the latter, and add that when he found it he also found that he could make good use of it by variously exploiting and emphasizing it. Instead of trying to ignore it or resolve it quickly, he let it almost seem to get the better of him. Out of his "failure" to unify what he was doing with words and what he was doing with actions he created the paradoxical success that is his dramatic art. Thus, if I sometimes sound as though I am saying he found the tension and sometimes as though I am claiming he introduced it, that is because the distinction is very difficult to make. Not that the tension doesn't always inform theatrical performance to some degree; rather that no artist of the theater makes quite the same use of it as Shakespeare.

In each of the chapters that follow I have addressed myself to a leading stylistic feature and a distinctive structural characteristic of the tragedy in question. These aspects tend again and again to be opposed, as if they belonged to different plays. Thus *Hamlet* is lavish in its use of language and remarkably thrifty in its approach to structure. *Othello* validates its hero with an important stylistic feature, the ability to narrate well, while reinforcing the power of its villain with an important structural advantage, namely, intimacy and complicity with the audience. *King Lear* opts for an unusually capacious design—geographically, generically, and symbolically enlarged—while also exploring the possibilities of an unusually intimate and inward style. And *Macbeth* makes a series of primitivistic structural choices and at the same time achieves an unusually sophisticated and complex poetry.

The oppositions sketched out by such terms as lavish and frugal, expansive and intimate, primitive and sophisticated, are of course approximations. Plays as complex as these can never be captured by simplified terminology or neat antinomies. They have too many crosscurrents and too rich a mix of theatrical potency and verbal suggestion. Once beyond what I hope is a useful alignment of Shakespeare's working habits and the natural tensions of theater, both in his time and more generally, my chapters tend to be more engrossed by the individual plays, by their distinctiveness and uniqueness, than by the temptation to herd them all into a little corral that I am overproud to have designed. It is gratifying, of course, to discover patterns that illuminate a great writer's thought processes and an artistic medium's deepest features and needs, but the emphasis and value of a study like this one must arrive where they began, with the perception of the astonishing dissimilarities among Shakespeare's major tragedies and indeed all of his plays. The groupings we use—problem comedy, formal period, late romance—help us to differentiate periods, phases, and lines of interest and emphasis. But Shakespeare is not bound by them, and we do well to remember that at all times.

Chapter One

Large Discourse
and Thrifty Action
in *Hamlet*

THE DILATING TEXT

A good place to begin consideration of *Hamlet* is with the question
of its size. The longest text (Q2, the second quarto) runs close to
four thousand lines, almost twice the length of *The Tempest* and
some 30 percent longer than the average Shakespearean tragedy.
Hamlet's playing time, uncut, is over four hours. Even if, as we
suspect, the full text wasn't played in Shakespeare's theater, the
play's sheer length must be said to send us some kind of signal.

What is signaled is its wordiness. *Hamlet* is talky. The characters
are much given to digressions, and the action to odd arrests and
apparent detours. Verbal elaboration is the norm, rather than the
exception. Even when the text is cut to a length more suitable for
performance we still have a play that both delights and bewilders
us with its brilliant prolixity, with the habit its characters have—
and the tragic hero, with his soliloquies, is only the most prominent
instance—of slowing or stopping the action while they discourse,
often at length, on matters that interest them, even when these are
not matters at hand.

This observation needs to be grounded in the historical context
of a theater where set pieces and what the French call *tirades* were

very popular. Elizabethan and Jacobean audiences liked plenty of action on the stage, but they also responded to stylistically ornate passages and long speeches the way opera-lovers respond to arias. Remarking the prolixity of *Hamlet*'s text, then, implies an unusual emphasis on a common tendency.

The term I propose to use for *Hamlet*'s stylistic elaborations is *dilations*. In this choice I differ from commentators who have explored the tendency before me. Francis Berry, for example, calls the soliloquies and set pieces *insets*, comparing a play to a gallery we walk through, with the verbal insets as hung pictures or statuary niches we periodically stop to inspect.[1] Bert States, in a brilliantly suggestive essay, calls them *word-pictures*. In *Hamlet*, he argues, one experiences "an almost encyclopedic procession of persons, animals, objects, processes, and instances from rural, professional, and household affairs, many of them strangely self-contained and portable, all spun out by the characters who . . . have an unusual habit of getting detained."[2]

Dilation, as I use it here, is an extremely inclusive term, taking in soliloquies, long speeches, narrative set pieces, digressions, and even shorter speeches that nevertheless act to "dilate" the text while slowing the progress of the action. I choose the term partly to avoid the sense that these elaborations are detours or superfluous ornamentations. Their "strangely self-contained and portable" quality is, I think, illusory. The speech the player recites about Pyrrhus is said to come from an old play, but the only play it comes from or belongs to is *Hamlet*. Nor would the tale of Ophelia's drowning or the "To be or not to be" soliloquy mean what they mean out of their context. These verbal elaborations appear detachable, but aren't. They belong to the *Hamlet* world as fully as any other element.

My term also has spatial implications, suggesting flexible expansions and contractions in the text. I prefer this to the more static pictorial suggestions of Berry and States. Dilation is also neutral enough to accommodate verbal amplification of all kinds and sizes, attempting to do justice to the play's remarkable stylistic diversity.

Finally, the whole idea of dilation can be linked, by a perfectly serious wordplay, to the tragic hero's popular reputation for indecisiveness. If Hamlet is such a dilatory revenger, the argument runs, perhaps it is because he inhabits such a dilated text![3]

The special frequency and peculiar aptness of the dilations in the *Hamlet* text can be established by a rapid survey of the first act. We will then be in a position to ask about kinds of dilations and recurring patterns and to undertake a consideration of the role of dilation in the play as a whole.

The action of scene 1 involves Horatio's visit to the platform, that he may see, and attempt to speak with, the ghost. His failure to do the latter leads to the resolve of Horatio and his companions to approach young Hamlet; the ghost, perhaps, will speak to him. There is first, then, a kind of failure of verbal dilation. The ghost spreads its arms but won't speak, even though Horatio seems to have a workable formula for addressing it. At the same time, the scene contains the following verbal elaborations: the story of the elder Hamlet's duel with old Fortinbras and the young Fortinbras's designs upon Denmark; a second narrative, from the well-read Horatio, about what went on in Rome just before Julius Caesar's assassination; a series of theoretical discussions about ghosts, beginning with "We do it wrong," moving to "I have heard / The cock" and on to "Some say that ever 'gainst that season comes," before resolving with a decision to act, "Let us impart." Narrating and theorizing, then, constitute the chief dilations here. The first use of narrative, "Last night of all, / When yond same star," is in fact interrupted by the ghost's appearance, as if by telling about something one might make it magically appear. The ghost is kinder to narrative the next time around, for he punctuates, without really interrupting, the Julius Caesar tale.

The theorizing passages in this scene form a linked series of dilations that take the audience, in three stages, further and further from the matter at hand, until the subject is Christmas and the nonappearance of ghosts, "so hallow'd and so gracious is that time."

The dilations create a sharp contrast to the action, a kind of cross-graining. They open the scope of the play's considerations to include history, politics, folklore, and religious belief, and they add a lyrical quality to a fundamentally perplexing experience.

The second scene opens with Claudius's capable but more predictable handling of royal business. His thirty-nine-line opening speech mixes theory with narrative and eventuates in the dispatching of Cornelius and Voltemand to Norway. It is a public elaboration upon decisions and actions already determined. The next dilation, by my count, is Hamlet's "Seems, madam?", an eleven-line response to his mother that, in turn, provokes thirty-one lines of advice from Claudius. Left alone, Hamlet delivers his first soliloquy, also of thirty-one lines, a mixture of narrative, theorizing, and passionate exclamation. He then hears, with frequent interruptions, the narrative of the ghost's appearances, and the scene closes with his decision to visit the platform that night.

These two scenes have been linked in a natural progression that would lead us to expect the platform visit to come next, but at this point the structure of the play dilates to make room for the scene of Laertes's leave-taking. The verbal dilations in this episode involve an extraordinary amount of advice: from Laertes to Ophelia on the subject of her relations with young Hamlet (forty-four lines); her brief retort (six lines) to the effect that Laertes should practice what he preaches; Polonius's delivery of a "few precepts" (twenty-four lines) that apparently recap what he was saying before the scene opened but that are tactfully characterized by Laertes as "a double blessing"; and Polonius's coarse and emphatic repetition of Laertes's advice about Hamlet when he has extracted from Ophelia the subject of her conversation with her brother. Just what the relation of all this advice to the future behavior of the characters will turn out to be, an audience cannot say, but it is clearly dilation of a peculiar and particular kind, something that runs in the family to a degree both comical and foreboding.

The two joined scenes that follow and conclude the act show no lessening of the tendencies to expansion and amplification thus far noted. Waiting for the ghost and explaining the Danish custom of carousal, Hamlet has time to extend that dilation into a theory of personality that has been seen as echoing the idea of the tragic flaw. His father's entrance cuts him off. His opening exhortation to the ghost requires nineteen lines. Horatio dilates on the unwisdom of following the beckoning ghost in a short speech (ten lines) on what might happen. When, in the scene that follows immediately, the ghost does come to speak, he proves a master dilator in his own right, despite his resolve at one point—"Brief let me be"—to make quick work of it. He dilates on a narrative he is not allowed to tell in terms of the effect it would have on the listener ("I could a tale unfold") before going on to the narrative of his murder, larding it with passionate exclamations, theoretical statements, and, of course, injunctions to revenge. Upon the ghost's departure, Hamlet has a seldom-noticed soliloquy of twenty-one lines in which he combines passionate utterance with self-injunctions and some theorizing of his own. He also takes thirteen lines to elaborate on his injunction when he swears his friends to secrecy. And so the first act closes.

While it is tricky to bring order to this delightful welter, this smorgasbord of stylistic amplifications, the dilations that have turned up in this survey of the play's first act seem to fall into four basic categories: narrative, injunctive, theoretical, and exclamatory. Moreover, it is possible to schematize them by means of Hamlet's later notion of the human capacity for *large discourse*. What defines large discourse is "looking before and after." In other words, narration, looking after, is fundamentally different from advice, prediction, command, prayer, and question, all of which can be grouped under the heading of injunction and all of which involve looking before, anticipating. Verbal dilation may be retrospective, and it may be prospective.

What if it is both? When discourse looks before *and* after and draws conclusions about prospects that are based on retrospects, it can be called theorizing. Has that an opposite? The opposite of *both* is *neither*. When discourse is incapable of looking beyond itself, is too mired in immediate circumstance, it becomes exclamation or ejaculation—outcries of pain, distress, wonder, or delight. It has forcefulness and immediacy, but it is limited to the present, one might even say blinded by it.

There are four basic directions, then, in which dilation may look. It may look backward, it may look ahead, it may rise to an overview of past and future, and it may sink down into present circumstances. The survey of act 1 identified clear-cut examples of each of these possibilities. Narration came first, and it was characterized by striking verbs and unforgettable images. Young Fortinbras, it is said, "Hath in the skirts of Norway here and there / Shark'd up a list of lawless resolutes." That is the recent past. Further back, we hear, "In the most high and palmy state of Rome, / A little ere the mightiest Julius fell, / The graves stood tenantless and the sheeted dead / Did squeak and gibber in the Roman streets" (1.1.116–19).[4] The past, it appears, was full of noises and of wild, mysterious activity. The fundamental fascination of storytelling is established in this play at the very outset. It will carry forward through "There is a willow grows askant the brook" and "Up from my cabin, / My sea-gown scarf'd about me, in the dark," right to the end, when looking before and looking after merge, as it were, in "And let me speak to th'yet unknowing world / How these things came about." Narration's noblest moment, in fact, lies beyond the play's close, when Horatio will draw his breath in pain in this harsh world to tell Hamlet's story.

The most obvious examples of "looking before" in our first act survey were the passages of advice: Claudius to Hamlet on how to deal with grief, Laertes to Ophelia on how to conduct her relationship with Hamlet, and Polonius, of course, to his son on how to live his whole life. But there are other ways of looking ahead. Claudius, explaining his policy, dispatches ambassadors. Horatio, and then Hamlet, enjoin the ghost to explain its presence, mixing interrogative with imperative, as in

Let me not burst in ignorance, but tell
Why thy canoniz'd bones, hearsed in death,

Have burst their cerements . . .

. . . .

. . . What may this mean,
That thou, dead corse, again in complete steel
Revisits thus the glimpses of the moon?

[1.4.44–46, 51–53]

And then, to be sure, the ghost, who comes with a stronger mission
than simply to advise, issues very specific instructions about the
future: Claudius is to be punished, Gertrude is to be spared. Already,
in the opening scenes, "looking before" through stylistic dilation
has come to have a variety of meanings—some of them comic and
apparently incidental, some of them absolutely crucial both to character and to plot.

When we look for theorizing in this part of the play, we recall
that the first scene drifted from narrative to theory as the conversation expanded to a musing on the ways of ghosts and of special
times when they can or cannot be abroad. Marcellus's lovely lines
show how the mind may move from single examples of past events
to a larger understanding based on temporal recurrence and thus
able to anticipate the future:

It faded on the crowing of the cock.
Some say that ever 'gainst that season comes
Wherein our Saviour's birth is celebrated,
This bird of dawning singeth all night long;
And then, they say, no spirit dare stir abroad,
The nights are wholesome, then no planets strike,
No fairy takes, nor witch hath power to charm,
So hallow'd and so gracious is that time.

[1.1.162–69]

This is cautious and wistful—as is Horatio's response, "So have I
heard and do in part believe it"—but it clearly moves to a vantage
point with regard to time that allows looking before and after at
once, a panorama that accumulates examples and, like Time itself

in Hotspur's definition, "takes survey of all the world." Its position "above" the action and the immediate present gives it a detachment that neither narrative nor injunction can fully claim. Again and again in this play, with varying degrees of confidence and success, characters as different as the gravedigger and the Player King will try to climb to the safer altitude of theory, only to fall back into the pell-mell action that defines their lives and circumstances. And Hamlet, just as he is the most imaginative enjoiner and narrator, will prove the ablest theorist, though he too will find theory cannot be sustained; like levitation, it would seem to be a minor and temporary miracle, a short triumph over one's earthbound condition.

Theorizing has its contrary too, a total absorption in the moment, expressed through phrases like "Fie on't, ah fie, 'tis an unweeded garden / That grows to seed; things rank and gross in nature / Possess it merely. That it should come to this!" There are touches of theory there, but the exclamation, and the emotional plummet from overview in phrases like "come to this," show how much the speaker is in effect pinned to his situation, unable to rise above it or even to look effectively before or after. There is a lot of this emotional plummeting in the first act, and its main sources are the younger and elder Hamlets, both of whom break down in the midst of attempts to narrate, anticipate, and theorize, reduced instead to cries of pain, anger, frustration, and despair:

> O all you host of heaven! O earth! What else?
> And shall I couple hell? O fie! Hold, hold, my heart,
> And you, my sinews, grow not instant old,
> But bear me stiffly up.
>
> [1.5.92–95]

The injunctions here are pinned to the present; they have no temporal perspective to speak of, but are about moment-to-moment survival. The passage follows by only a few lines the father's own outcry, "O horrible! O horrible! most horrible!" It can be objected that these outcries are not large discourse at all, but disruptions of it, breakings off from narrative or injunction or theory, and that is quite true. But they *are* dilations, verbal expansions, and they constitute, in relation to the schema of backward, forward, and up, a fourth possibility, down, a sinking into emotional absorption quite painfully lodged in an immediate present.

If the four kinds of dilation sometimes exist in pure form in the first act, they are at least as often mingled, to impressive effect, in what seem like inextricable combinations. This is scarcely surprising: if the mind and voice can choose deliberately to face this way or that, they can also, especially under duress, glance wildly about, three or four ways in effect, almost at once. Here is an example:

> Heaven and earth,
> Must I remember? Why, she would hang on him
> As if increase of appetite had grown
> By what it fed on; and yet within a month—
> Let me not think on't—Frailty, thy name is woman—
> A little month, or ere those shoes were old
> With which she follow'd my poor father's body,
> Like Niobe, all tears—why, she—
> O God, a beast that wants discourse of reason
> Would have mourn'd longer.
>
> [1.2.142-51]

This runs rapidly from exclamation into narrative, with a glance toward theorizing, back to exclamation, once more to theory phrased as ejaculation ("Frailty, thy name is woman"), into narrative again, once more interrupted by exclamation and theoretical assertion ("O God, a beast that wants discourse of reason / Would have mourn'd longer"). Such is the texture of the wonderful first soliloquy. It has been praised as realistically broken utterance, the portrait of a mind almost unhinged by emotional stress, but the schema for dilations shows that there is also a kind of wild bouncing among discursive possibilities—now back to the event Hamlet would rather not reiterate to himself, now up toward an attempt to understand its meaning, only to be hauled abruptly down to a pained entrapment in present emotion. Although the speech finally resolves itself in prediction and self-injunction ("It is not, nor it cannot come to good. / But break my heart, for I must hold my tongue"), the apparent opportunity to take a new direction is countered by the ironic smothering of any possibility for action or speech that will move the speaker out of his eternal present: he seems doomed to painful recollection and ricocheting among mental and verbal dilations that afford neither true understanding nor emotional relief.

Like son, we could say, like father. Here is the ghost, in much the same vein:

> O wicked wit, and gifts that have the power
> So to seduce!—won to his shameful lust
> The will of my most seeming-virtuous queen.
> O Hamlet, what a falling off was there,
> From me, whose love was of that dignity
> That it went hand in hand even with the vow
> I made to her in marriage, and to decline
> Upon a wretch whose natural gifts were poor
> To those of mine.
> But virtue, as it never will be mov'd,
> Though lewdness court it in the shape of heaven,
> So lust, though to a radiant angel link'd,
> Will sate itself in a celestial bed
> And prey on garbage.
> But soft, methinks I scent the morning air:
> Brief let me be. Sleeping within my orchard . . .
>
> [1.5.44–59]

Again, everything is here in rapid succession—most briefly injunction, as self-address, though injunction is in fact the main aim of the ghost's discourse. Attempts at narration and injunction, interrupted by theorizing on the one hand and emotional outbursts on the other, help link the minds and imaginations of the two Hamlets. These attempts constitute a less coherent form of discourse than that Polonius employs in addressing his son with wise saws and modern instances or than the careful narratives of Horatio, but they also suggest capacities for large discourse that are impressive in their nimbleness and moving in the pain their rapidity articulates. What I have called the "plummet" from theoretical overview to emotional collapse, from seeing before and after to seeing nothing but a painful present fact, is an especially impressive feature of this play; earlier Shakespearean sufferers, such as Richard II or Romeo or even Brutus, were lazy floaters up and down in comparison to Hamlet, who rises and falls with dispatch along a philosophical and emotional spectrum.

All this activity, even if it is mainly discursive and imagined, helps explain our impression that a great deal has happened in the first act. The dilations, rightly seen, have not really interrupted or slowed the action. They eventuate, again and again, in resolves to act, for instance:

> Let us impart what we have seen tonight
> Unto young Hamlet ...

> I shall in all my best obey you, madam.

> I'll speak to it though hell itself should gape ...

> I shall the effect of this good lesson keep
> As watchman to my heart.

> Look to't, I charge you. Come your ways.

> By heaven, I'll make a ghost of him that lets me.
> I say away. —Go on, I'll follow thee.

> *Swear by his sword.*

> > Let us go in together.
> And still your fingers to your lips, I pray.

These resolves have their problematic aspects, but they suggest a constant interaction of looking before and after, up and down, with the need to move forward in time, to decide and to act. The play is dilatory in its incessant tendencies to dilation, but not in the other, negative sense of the word. It does not dawdle or sprawl or lose energy; it plunges forward in a purposeful and exhilarating fashion.

Perhaps it is by now a truism that Hamlet's indecisive and delaying ways have been much exaggerated, on the basis of his own self-condemnations more than on evidence in the plot. It is also something of a truism that a revenge play needs delay if it is to achieve length and interest. A few years ago I proposed that Hamlet could be seen as a character who tries to rewrite and redirect the unfashionable revenge play he finds himself cast in.[5] That is not yet a truism, but I do not intend to abandon it here, just to modify it with the notion that even if these other qualifications to Hamlet's supposed weakness of character were not present, we might still be able to understand why and how he is dilatory by recognizing the dilating style of the play and the dilated world that results. One can imagine plays in which situation necessitates narrative dilation, *or* a lot of injunction, *or* a lot of emotional outpouring, *or* a number of attempts at a theoretical understanding of events. We will find such emphases among the other three tragedies to be discussed in this study. To see that we have in *Hamlet* a play in which all of these regularly occur—sometimes in distinct form, sometimes remarkably intermingled—is to be able to place and understand the drama more clearly and more firmly. The preceding definition and description of the dilating tendencies in *Hamlet* constitutes a partial map of style that may help us find our way around in the rest of the play. It is time to venture beyond the first act and suggest some ways in which the four kinds of dilation and their interaction may help to clarify and integrate parts of the play that have troubled interpreters and performers.

We can begin by noting that the characters themselves are often aware of the dilations that surround them, sometimes to comic effect. "This is too long," says Polonius of the First Player's speech, a case of pot criticizing kettle if ever there was one. Sometimes, like a poor actor, Polonius requires prompting and direction in his own dilations; Reynaldo must help him find his place on the subject of how to spy on Laertes, and Gertrude, in a miniaturized version of her son's advice to the players, asks him for "more matter with less art," though to little avail. Someone else, as States remarks, might well have said the same thing to *her* on the occasion of her report on Ophelia's drowning, but who cuts off a queen?[26] The one character seemingly capable of curbing his own dilations is Hamlet, who breaks off his description to Horatio of the kind of man he can admire with an embarrassed "something too much of this." At other times, though, he even disregards sensible warnings, like Horatio's " 'Twere to consider too curiously to consider so," and plunges on into dilations we may recognize as "too curious" but listen to quite happily anyway.

Another possibility is that dilations may occur within dilations, like interrupted interruptions, little cadenzas or flourishes. Gertrude, in the midst of her account of Ophelia's drowning, allows herself a short digression on the alternative names for "long purple": "That liberal shepherds give a grosser name, / But our cold maids do dead men's fingers call them" (4.7.169–70). In one sense, of course, this is not to the purpose at all; it cuts across the pathos. Nor is it to the character; Gertrude seems an unlikely collector of alternative folknames for wildflowers. But in another sense it is wonderfully apt. We have seen Ophelia distributing her collected flowers and herbs, identifying them as she does, and we have seen the language of liberal shepherds breaking through the speech of the cold maid overcome by madness. We also know something about Gertrude's liberality, and know too that Ophelia is now "cold" in a more literal sense. Gertrude interrupts herself to better effect than she can possibly realize.

Hamlet's tale of the pirates, while basically a narrative, has some crucial subdilations as well. One is his remark about the divinity that shapes our ends, rough-hew them how we will. Another is a metaphor from the world of theater—"Or I could make a prologue to my brains, / They had begun the play" (5.2.30–31)—a strange observation for a hero who is supposed to be conscious of his guilt in delaying his revenge. And then there is room for two parodies

21

of the inflated style of court documents, first in the paraphrase Hamlet offers of the letter from Claudius—"an exact command, / Larded with many several sorts of reasons / Importing Denmark's health, and England's too, / With ho! such bugs and goblins in my life"—and then again in the substitute he writes, out-dilating his uncle's royal style of injunction:

> An earnest conjuration from the King,
> As England was his faithful tributary,
> As love between them like the palm might flourish,
> As peace should still her wheaten garland wear
> And stand a comma 'tween their amities,
> And many such-like 'as'es of great charge . . .
>
> [5.2.38–43]

The fun of this lies partly in the fact that court-inflated language will shortly make its appearance in the brainless, ornate person of Osric, as if Hamlet's parody had given birth to a character through sheer exuberance. His wrapping of things in rawer breath will always have these splendid foils: kill a Polonius and an Osric will mushroom up to take his place. Then too, in the midst of our enjoyment is the special knowledge that colors our understanding of the encounter: our intuition that it is Osric who brings Hamlet the invitation that will take him to his doom. The mixed response that results sounds, once more, the special note of *Hamlet,* its distinctive and mysterious tone.

A refined sense of how the dilations work is helpful with the soliloquies, too. We have already seen how deliberately Hamlet's first soliloquy mixes narrative, injunction, theory, and exclamation. Its dominant note, however, is the exclamatory, to which it keeps returning, and that dominance is signalled by the opening line, where injunction turns to exclamation through an emphasis on present anguish: "O that this too too sullied flesh would melt" (1.2.129). If we turn to other soliloquies now, we see that Shakespeare uses this same strong signal for the exclamatory note in the next two soliloquies by his hero, as follows: "O all you host of heaven! O earth! What else?" (the "unnoticed" soliloquy near the end of act 1) and, of course, "O what a rogue and peasant slave am I," after the First Player's speech. The same "signal" is used for the speech by Ophelia that begins "O, what a noble mind is here o'erthrown!" (3.1.151), one seldom mentioned as a soliloquy but necessarily viewed that way in context. (She's addressing either herself or the audience, or both, not someone else on stage.) The "O" signal also marks the beginning of Claudius's remarkable self-communing after the performance of *The Murder of Gonzago,* the soliloquy that begins, "O, my offence is rank, it smells to heaven" (3.3.36). What better way to mark speeches of mediation and self-communion than by opening them with the vowel that of all others sounds the note of exclamation? Yet one does not find it in the major soliloquies of the other tragedies, this "O" signal. It is a convention unique to *Hamlet.*

Shakespeare also creates the convention in order to be able to depart from it. If three of Hamlet's soliloquies (as well as one each by Ophelia and Claudius) begin with "O" and sound the dominance of exclamation, there are three more that do not. "To be or not to be" is of course the best known, and it is often remarked how much more tranquil and theoretical than the others it is, a consideration of suicide as a possibility and of fear of death as a disabling influence in human activities of all kinds that is remarkably detached in tone. This speech is able to sustain its theoretical height quite successfully, and we feel the difference. Actors playing Hamlet have sometimes chosen to carry a book in this scene, to suggest that the speech is provoked by some philosophical passage he has been reading, and everyone wonders, of course, whether Ophelia is an auditor, since she is clearly on stage somewhere. She seems to be praying at the back, or reading to herself, and conventionally out of earshot. In any case, when this speech is done well, it makes us feel that we are somehow at the center of the play, as one might be at the eye of a storm, with all of the issues spread before us in a less anguished mood than we have seen before or are likely to see again.

Another soliloquy by Hamlet that does not begin with the powerful exclamatory "O" is the one in which he contemplates the praying Claudius and decides, in twenty-four considered lines, to wait for another time to kill him (3.3.73–96). It seems important to Shakespeare to signal that this is *not* a moment of great mental anguish or indecision. Those who try to read it as such are ignoring the different ways in which the dilations in *Hamlet* are handled. The soliloquy does not bounce wildly among three or four possibilities of discourse, but rather maintains a theoretical, and thus contemplative, tone fairly successfully. It is much more kindred to "To be or not to be" than to the soliloquies beginning, "O."

The final soliloquy in this survey is Hamlet's fourth-act speech following his glimpse of Fortinbras's army (4.4.32–66); it begins in a mildly exclamatory fashion but moves readily to a theoretical level and is largely successful at staying there. There is self-accusation in the speech, but it is not agonized, and Hamlet's relative peace of mind is signalled by the lack of abruptly shifting discourse. It looks as though Shakespeare sets up a style of rebounding discourse as an index of mental agony in *Hamlet,* using the tragic hero and the other characters as well, and then partially frees his hero from it for the second half of the play. Hamlet has lapses into agony in the second half, but they come in the presence of, and in response to, the words and actions of other characters, for example, of Laertes at Ophelia's grave. When alone, he is able to sustain a remarkably contemplative way of looking at the world and at his problematic place in it. An actor playing the part, or a director, might find that information useful.

An enhanced understanding of the textual dilations helps with the players, too. They have no sooner arrived than Hamlet, looking backward, asks for the recitation of a speech from an old play; he himself can remember its beginning (2.2.446–60), and the First Player is able to recall the whole thing, a remarkable feat of memory (2.2.464–514). The speech has many associations, including a reminder of the period and style of the *Ur-Hamlet,* when Senecan revenge tragedy seemed less absurd, but for our purposes the notable thing about it is that it is a narrative, a dilation that had a clear function in its own text and occupies a more dubious position in this one, since it is both stylistically and structurally less germane to the drama at hand. It reminds us of a traditional function that narrative serves in drama, to report a crucial offstage event, the kind of thing that will have more supple representations in Gertrude's report of Ophelia's drowning and Hamlet's account of his sea-journey and the pirates. It reminds us, in fact, of the difference between set piece and dilation.

From an interruption that combines exclamation and injunction:

> Out, out, thou strumpet Fortune! All you gods
> In general synod take away her power,
> Break all the spokes and fellies from her wheel,
> And bowl the round nave down the hill of heaven
> As low as to the fiends
>
> [2.2.489–93]

it turns back to narrative and the pathos of Hecuba's grief, ending with the tears in the eyes of the performer that astonish Polonius and trigger Hamlet's soliloquy a moment later.

The next time we see the players we have moved from looking after to looking before: Hamlet is serving up an extensive set of injunctions to them, in the form of his famous advice (3.2.1–45). Since this calm dilation follows the "sweet bells jangled out of tune" of his tirades to Ophelia, it leads us to suspect—especially as an amateur is proposing to advise professionals on their craft—that Hamlet has been doing more acting than we had realized. His discourse mixes in some narrative ("O there be players that I have seen play ... have so strutted and bellowed that I have thought some of Nature's journeymen made men, and not made them well, they imitated nature so abominably") and, with his famous aesthetic principle of "the mirror up to nature," a certain amount of theory, but first and last it is advice on acting and playing, and it joins the passages of notable injunction from earlier in the play, mostly from Claudius, the Ghost, and Polonius, to the set of injunctions Hamlet will shortly deliver to his mother in her chamber.

The narrative of Pyrrhus from the old play showed a stable relation of past to present. The advice we hear Hamlet giving the players suggests a stable relation of theory to practice, present and past to future. When we come to the actual performance of *The Murder of Gonzago,* however, the predictable elements begin to unsettle and shift around. It is true that the main object of the performance, a dramatized narrative dilation of Claudius's crime intended to make him acknowledge it in the present, appears to have been achieved. The king rises, calls for light, and breaks off the play. He does not proclaim his malefactions, as Hamlet had suggested he might, but Hamlet's elation certainly confirms his sense of the success of the device. Yet we are left with some unanswered questions. The largest one has to do with the way the players chose to present their material. Although a successful performance would seem to depend especially on the element of surprise, they dilate upon what is to come, confusing narrative and prediction, in the form of a dumb show! (By doing this they have, it is true, given occupation to generations of commentators, and perhaps that is enough.) This dumb show reminds us of two other moments of pantomime—the ghost spreading its arms, and Hamlet visiting Ophelia as she sits sewing in her closet—and shows that dilation need not be verbal. Still, it seems both as needless and as destructive to suspense as was the prologue of the mechanicals in *A Midsummer Night's Dream,* marking a level of professional ineptitude in this group of players that seems to justify any anxiety suggested by Hamlet's advice. If the dumb show is wide of the players' and Hamlet's purpose, however, it can be said to serve Shakespeare's well enough. The audience of *Hamlet,* knowing exactly what is to come, can fix their attention on Claudius and regain the suspense that the overexplicit prologue has dissipated.

The whole episode of the players, along with a number of other events in the midsection of the play, may be seen as a structural dilation, a slowing-down of action and forward movement while questions of interest—in this case questions that are remarkably reflective to the dramatic medium itself—are investigated and discussed. The process delays the revenge but multiplies our perspectives on it.

The graveyard scene is probably the most surprising structural dilation in the play. It seems deliberately intended to contrast with the first-act interview with the ghost, even to the visual pun in Shakespeare's theater of using the trapdoor a second time. The ways in which its dilations are retrospective of earlier events in the play are manifold, but two examples may suffice here. The first is quite minor—it is a bit of facetious injunction to the skull of Yorick:

> Now get you to my lady's chamber and tell her, let her paint an inch thick, to this favour she must come. Make her laugh at that.
> [5.1.186–89]

This is intriguing for the way it recalls things said by Hamlet to Ophelia about cosmetics (echoed by Claudius in his "harlot's cheek" confessional aside) and to Gertrude about counterfeit appearances, and visits to the two ladies' chambers and closets, one narrated and one staged, but it is also intriguing as a piece of injunction that cannot be other than hypothetical. At the graveyard looking before and looking after cease to have separate meanings. In that sense, the moment anticipates the play's ending, where, as noted earlier, narrative and injunction also come together, along with theory and exclamation.

In terms of dilations and their history in the play, the other striking aspect of the graveyard scene is the way in which Hamlet is pulled down from his contemplative and theoretical "considering too curiously" to a world of pained and entrapped exclamation by the arrival of the funeral cortege and by his wild response to Laertes's dilations, injunctive and exclamatory, on the subject of his sister's death. The struggle in the grave is a physical version of the mental process we saw enacted over and over in the soliloquies, the "fall" from narrative, injunction, and contemplative detachment and a subsequent contraction of the mind around an intense preoccupation with the present, whether in wonder or joy or, more often, in rage, grief, and despair. It is exhilarating to have that movement reified, as well as a sharp reminder that Hamlet's new-won detachment is and must continue to be a precarious thing. Muse as you will on skulls and bones, it seems to say, you cannot fully withdraw from action: plot will have its day, dilation must be set aside, readiness is all.

In one of John Donne's Holy Sonnets, a speaker who feels trapped in time and bewildered by circumstance prays to his creator for relief:

> Thou hast made me. And shall thy worke decay?
> Repaire me now, for now mine end doth haste,
> I runne to death, and death meets me as fast,
> And all my pleasures are like yesterday;
> I dare not move my dimme eyes any way,
> Despaire behind, and death before doth cast
> Such terrour, and my feeble flesh doth waste
> By sinne in it, which it t'wards hell doth weigh;
> Onely thou art above, and when towards thee
> By thy leave I can looke, I rise againe;
> But our old subtle foe so tempteth me,
> That not one houre my selfe I can sustaine;
> Thy Grace may wing me to prevent his art,
> And thou like Adamant draw mine iron heart.[7]

Here are our four directions once again: a past that tends to produce despair, a future that holds only mortality, a weight of flesh and chthonic drag that can only be countered by a rising up to heights of contemplation and spiritual detachment. It is interesting, as an experiment, to make the speaker a dramatic hero, addressing the playwright. The substitution allows us to ask whether the prayer can be answered in profane and dramaturgical terms. Obviously, on one level, if the plot of *Hamlet* is to complete itself, the prayer must be ignored. But insofar as it is listened to and temporarily granted, delays and dilations are possible in which the hero rises toward the condition and understanding of his creator, who is of course always "above," able to look before and after. This is one

way of saying what we already know: that Hamlet is a more philosophical tragic hero than Othello, Lear, Macbeth, Coriolanus, Antony, or Cleopatra; that he cannot sustain himself very long at a
theoretical and contemplative level; and that he does so at the grace
of his maker, who allows him to dilate the text and slow the action,
giving him wings, as it were ("Thy Grace may wing me"), by his
inspiration. It is one way of accounting for our sense of miraculous
creation in this play, a quality that is surely related to speculations
about the temperamental intimacy between author and tragic hero.

Another way of getting at this special quality is to talk about the
mysterious sense of exhilaration with which the play closes. Hamlet
has, we must admit, succeeded more or less by accident; he leaves
a tremendous mess behind, and a great many unanswered questions.
What is more, his kingdom is about to fall into the hands of an
unimaginative Norwegian opportunist. And yet we are elated. Horatio has no other wish than to die with his friend, but he is forbidden
that privilege and ordered to remain alive so that he may tell Hamlet's story and bring some order to the final confusion. That delights
us too.

Something of what is happening at the close must be related to
the fact that narration, always a stabilizing element in the world of
Hamlet, is joining itself to injunction, prediction, anticipation—the
whole proleptic cast that has so bedeviled the plot and characters.
A play's or story's close completes it and thus makes its retelling
or re-enacting a continual possibility. Hamlet lives, in that sense,
to die and then to live again, a kind of phoenix. We can also note
that theory and exclamation join hands as the play ends around the
central fact of death as a release from time and as the cancellation
of a condition in which large discourse and experience were unable
to have identical meanings and aims. Listen to Hamlet, responding
to Laertes's dying request that they exchange words of forgiveness,
an exchange that will combine past and future if "Mine and my
father's death come not upon thee, / Nor thine on me":

Heaven make thee free of it. I follow thee.
I am dead, Horatio. Wretched Queen, adieu.

You that look pale and tremble at this chance,
That are but mutes or audience to this act,
Had I but time—as this fell sergeant, Death,
Is strict in his arrest—O, I could tell you—
But let it be.

[5.2.337–43]

The four directions of dilation mingle here, not wildly as in some
of the soliloquies, but tranquilly and satisfyingly. It is remarkable
how four such simple words as "but let it be" can seem an appropriate point of arrival for a play of such stylistic complexity. The
same notes are struck in Hamlet's next two speeches—"the rest is
silence" has the same direct simplicity—as if to reassure us that
this sense of resolution is not ephemeral but firm and inevitable.
Hamlet becomes identical with his story, and if its closure is his
death, so it is also the end of contrary stylistic impulses, the closure
of all dilations. And the fact that the story can and will be retold is
both his hope of vindication and his chance to live again.

ECONOMIES OF STRUCTURE

Expressing disgust at the rapidity of his mother's remarriage, Hamlet makes a bitter joke about household economies:

Thrift, thrift, Horatio. The funeral bak'd meats
Did coldly furnish forth the marriage tables.

[1.2.180–81]

If his hero had little regard for "leftovers," Shakespeare seems to
have dined on them quite contentedly in putting his great play
together. The attractions of making one thing serve two purposes
and of employing stale or overused materials led him to effects of
concentration that feel very different from the exuberant inventions
of the play's language. He returned to a dubious and unfashionable
subgenre, Senecan revenge tragedy, and he appears to have re-
written or adapted an old play by Thomas Kyd. Nor was this re-

sorting to used materials his only thrift. He also contrived to make the dramatic medium turn back and comment upon itself in unprecedented ways. Dramatic reflexivity as a kind of shortcut to meaning, a concentrating device, had been tried before, but never so fully or effectively. Finally, within the dramatic action Shakespeare showed himself willing to recycle situations and stage-effects in ways that are sometimes quite startling.

Taken together, the structural recyclings of *Hamlet* bespeak a tendency that both matches and opposes its prolix and dilated style. The matching comes from our sense of labyrinthine complexity of structure. But mazes, we must remind ourselves, have a certain kind of economy as well. They use space efficiently by means of concentrated repetition. They bewilder us by rhythmic resort to the same effects again and again. They appear to multiply structure without resort to new materials. Another helpful analogy comes in the practice that folklorists call *nesting*. The same object or pattern recurs within itself, on a smaller scale. A play within a play is probably the most obvious example of such a practice in the realm of theater. It is an elaboration, but we must also be struck by the thrift it implies. If we thought *Hamlet* a collaboration, we might well conjecture a partnership between a verbal spendthrift, bent on novelty and abundance of invention, and a thrifty plotter, cunningly reusing the same few, apparently threadbare, ideas. The contrast may well be deliberate, creating as it does a paradoxical texture and a sense of creative impulses that effectively counterbalance each other.

Seneca was of course the one classical tragedian whose works were widely known in Elizabethan England and thus available as models for contemporary playwrights, but by the time Shakespeare came to *Hamlet,* Seneca's emphasis on violent acts of revenge—imitated in the popular experiments of Marlowe, Kyd, and Shakespeare in the late 1580s and early 1590s—had become something of a joke. We do not know whether John Marston's decadent and parodic treatment of the genre in *Antonio's Revenge,* written for a children's company, actually preceded or followed Shakespeare's

Hamlet, but either way the effect is the same: a genre which had been employed straightforwardly ten years earlier now looked so primitive that it was apt to be treated as something of a joke when it was broached at all.[8] Ben Jonson tells us that people could still be found who would swear that Kyd's *Spanish Tragedy* and Shakespeare's own early *Titus Andronicus* were "the best plays yet," but that of course is precisely an acknowledgment of their obsolescence.[9] Seneca's influence can be found in Shakespeare's *Richard III,* but by *Romeo and Juliet* it has faded away, and Shakespeare's return to the genre of tragedy in *Julius Caesar,* while it might have marked a resurgence of the Senecan manner, given the subject and the Roman playwright's theoretical eminence, scarcely feels Senecan at all. In taking on the theme of *Hamlet,* then, Shakespeare would appear to be like a playwright who resorts to odd plots as an excuse to mount his new poetry, too inventive as to style, too uninventive as to story. Or perhaps he should be compared to a gravedigger, pulling old bones from a place where they had rested undisturbed for a decade.

Indeed, like the gravedigger identifying the skull of Yorick, we think we can say whose these bones are. The existence of a dramatic version of the Hamlet story, commonly referred to as the *Ur-Hamlet* and very likely to have been written by Thomas Kyd, is virtually undisputable, which means of course that Shakespeare was not reviving simply an old style and subgenre, but a specific example of it.[10] In fact, the references to the *Ur-Hamlet,* the earliest of which is dated 1589, are testimony not only to its existence but also to its popularity, and it would appear that Kyd, in writing *The Spanish Tragedy,* which survives, and the *Ur-Hamlet,* unhappily lost, created two of the most popular plays of his generation, plays which had in common their successful transference of the characteristics and preoccupations of Senecan revenge tragedy to the contemporary English stage.

Attempts to reconstruct Kyd's play are of course conjectural, but we know that there was an entreating ghost, crying out from under the stage "Hamlet, revenge." That fact suggests in turn that the hero needed either reminding or encouragement, or both. As I have contended elsewhere, this connection to the old play lends an extraordinary tension to Hamlet's interview with his father and may help account for his subsequent behavior when the ghost cries out from under the stage, "Swear" and "Swear by his sword."[11] The likelihood that these moments would strongly remind the audience of the older play suggests why Hamlet can make jocular references to the ghost as "old mole" and "this fellow in the cellarage": he is openly acknowledging a theatrical cliche. I have argued elsewhere that an interpretation of Hamlet's character and behavior may be partly shaped by those facts, but the point here is simply that the reuse not only of the old play but of some of its most notorious moments is acknowledged, rather than concealed. Shakespeare wants his audience to recall, not only that they are seeing an old legend dramatized and a no-longer-fashionable dramatic style renovated, but also that they are seeing a once-popular play revived and transformed, with some of its most familiar features intact.

Since Kyd's extant example of Senecan revenge tragedy features a good deal of speechifying and a marked delay in carrying out the revenge, we may suspect that those are characteristics of Shakespeare's *Hamlet* chiefly because they were features of the *Ur-Hamlet*. Hieronimo's difficulties in accomplishing revenge in *The Spanish Tragedy* stem from a combination of practical problems and periodic madness; that does not of course mean that the problems of Kyd's Hamlet were identical. We are not free to assume that the entreating ghost existed either to point out an enfeebled will of the sort that Hamlet is traditionally supposed to suffer from or to underline the kind of frustration and derangement that Hieronimo experiences. The theatrical device is effective in either case, and the fact that one hero is a son attempting to revenge a father and the other a father attempting to revenge a son shows us that Kyd went in for variations as much as he did for repetitions. Whatever went on in Kyd's version, we know that Shakespeare's hero is revisited only once by the ghost, who says he comes to "whet" his son's "blunted purpose." Hamlet has, against instructions, turned from pursuing Claudius to reviling Gertrude. The accusations of delay stem mostly from Hamlet himself. I think few readers or spectators wholly blame or wholly exonerate Hamlet's actions and inactions, but the fact that he was a very contemporary-seeming individual entrapped in a situation that was clearly old-fashioned must have been part of his original audience's perception of his dilemma. That he tries to rewrite the script and redirect the action is scarcely surprising, and that he eventually accepts the plot and his part in it is also easy to understand. What needs noting here is that Shakespeare used the very fact of the age and familiarity of the revenge tragedy to enact some of the most central meanings of his version and to shape his hero's unique character and consciousness. We can be thrilled by novelty and invention; we can also be thrilled by an economy of means, the stale and overfamiliar transformed by a simple shift of context and emphasis. If one can imagine Ben Jonson muttering, "Why would he want to rewrite that old story?" one can also imagine him saying, in grudging admiration, "Oh, that's why!"

The pattern we are looking at is familiar to anyone acquainted with Shakespeare's artistic practice. His recognition that theatrical art combines the familiar and the surprising had already led him to experiment with dramatic mixtures of old and new, and would continue to be a preoccupation in his late work, right to the end. I have elsewhere described *The Tempest* as an attempt to respond to the theatrical innovations represented by Jonson's *The Alchemist* without discarding the values represented by Marlowe's *Doctor Faustus*.[12] No playwright was more original and daring than Shakespeare, but repudiation of artists who had preceded him and of literary fashions that were apparently stale was not a necessary adjunct to his sense of his own artistry. The art of the past could be reborn in the present. Slavish imitation of models was unacceptable, but the durability of certain themes and styles, despite changes of fashion, was fascinating to contemplate. Why had the ghost and the dilemma of the revenger proved so popular when brought to the English stage by Kyd? To write *Hamlet* by rewriting the *Ur-Hamlet* was a way to ask and answer that question. And as Shakespeare achieved in the process his greatest and most memorable tragedy, the argument for combining recognition of the durability of popular art with the need for imaginative transformation of it would seem to be compelling indeed.

To say that Shakespeare made his audience conscious from time to time of the new play's deliberate building upon the old one is to have entered the realm of theatricality and artistic reflexivity, the second major area of *Hamlet*'s structural thrift. I am scarcely the first to broach this complex topic.[13] The stress I wish to give the discussion here is that *Hamlet*'s use of its own medium to create and clarify its meanings is another stroke of thrift by the playwright, one that lies at the very heart of his accomplishments. Certainly no attempt to describe the shortcuts and nestings of *Hamlet*'s structure would be complete without some investigation of the self-conscious use of theater through the arrival of the players, the quotation of a speech from an old play, a preperformance discussion of the art of acting, and the performance of a play-within-the-play. Nor can we afford to ignore the way that our recognition of acting and role-playing spreads from these centers of theatrical and dramatic reflexivity to encompass most of the characters and much of the action.

We can begin a consideration of theatricality by noting that the connection between the company of players and the play-within-the-play is more a convenience than a necessity. Hamlet could have staged a play to accomplish his end without using professional actors, as is indeed the case in *The Spanish Tragedy,* where Hieronimo is able to carry out his plans precisely because the performance is an amateur occasion that he directs and acts in. Conversely, a group of actors could have visited Elsinore and provoked some talk about the theater and some impromptu recitation without going on to stage a dramatic performance. While it makes compelling sense to connect the actors and the performance, separating them temporarily helps to isolate different effects they have on the play.

First, then, the play that is performed in act 3. It's important to recognize that Shakespeare need not have introduced a traveling company of professional players into Elsinore to stage a performance. There is nothing about the occasion, including the preliminary advice Hamlet gives to the cast, that might not just as well have involved amateurs. The play gives Claudius an image of his guilt and satisfies Hamlet, both as a device of detection and as confirmation of the ghost's word, but nothing about it, from its inept dumb show, to its decorous and wooden couplets, to the overacting suggested by Hamlet's impatient interruption ("Begin, murderer. Leave thy damnable faces and begin." [3.2.246–47]), marks it as the work of professionals and contemporaries. We can produce explanations for these anomalies—for instance, that Hamlet has made the players dredge up an old bad play in order to obtain a present plot-fit to Claudius's murder, or that the prologue is intended to let the audience of *Hamlet* know the overall shape of something they will be able to watch only a fragment of, or that Elsinorean taste is way behind that of Wittenberg—but the fact remains that professional actors are neither suggested by, nor necessary to, the series of events involving the performance of *The Murder of Gonzago* in act 3.

The scene in which the players arrive, in act 2, on the other hand, puts unusual stress on their profession and its characteristic rewards and hardships. We learn that the actors are traveling because of a ban on their playing in the city, and we hear that they have become less popular because of the rivalry of a children's company. We hear Polonius describe their abilities and summarize their repertory, probably from a handbill, with some elaborations of his own, and we meet them individually. Then comes the impressive piece of recitation from a play that is both out of fashion and a little too austere to have been widely accepted. Hamlet confers briefly with the chief player on the "command performance" he has already conceived and goes on to a soliloquy comparing the player's manufactured passion with his own "dull and muddy-mettled" response to his situation.

This series of discussions and events adds up to a portrait of the acting profession and its contemporary characteristics that is surprisingly detailed and realistic. Shakespeare may well, as various commentators have conjectured, have added the passage about the children's company as an afterthought, but it is scarcely a surprising addition to the discussion of "the profession," merely coming as the most contemporary reference of all. When Hamlet praises the old play by saying that "there were no sallets in the lines to make the matter savoury, nor no matter in the phrase that might indict the author of affection," he is already glancing at playwrights like Marston who were trying to rival his accomplishment and attract audiences away from his company. The issue of what constituted good drama and good acting at the very moment of *Hamlet*'s writing and performance could not be more directly raised. As in the attitude toward old materials implied by the choice of the *Ur-Hamlet* and the out-of-fashion Senecan revenge play, we seem to have Shakespeare arguing here for an attitude toward the past that eschews simple repudiation and one toward the present that is skeptical of novelty for its own sake.

Again, many of these matters could have been aired without leading to the play that is staged in act 3, though we would surely have been disappointed to see actors and no performance. But Shakespeare leaves us to sort out many of the questions raised by discrepancies between what we see in act 2 and in act 3. He gives us a kind of scrambled history of drama in his time, from the first clumsy dumb shows and rhymed verse, to the majestic but verbose Senecanism of Marlowe and Kyd, right up to the current fashion for decadent plots acted by children, and he lets us determine *Hamlet*'s relation to all of that by inference. The effect is subtler than if he had simply stressed the archaic and amateur on the one hand or the contemporary and fashionable on the other, but it is also more bewildering.

The bridge, or rather perhaps the tower from which we survey this terrain, would seem to be Hamlet's speech of advice to the players, since he not only reviews changes of acting style but also offers aesthetic theory to support his own preferences (3.2.1–53). He argues for a realistic art, based on mimesis, and if this isn't altogether consistent with his fondness for the rugged Pyrrhus speech, it does, on the whole, make sense given what we know of his character. He dislikes overacting, on the ground that it distorts the mimetic function of drama. What complicates his position that playing holds "the mirror up to nature" is that his is a discussion of the mirror's value offered from within the mirror, an action that both exemplifies and considers (reflects upon?) the value of its exemplification. Presumably the value of theater, not excluding the appropriate style of acting he is calling for, was (and should always be) simultaneously defined and illustrated by the actor playing Hamlet. This simultaneity is *thrift* in a very special sense. It allows us to consider the value and effectiveness of this play in relation to all other available examples, past and present, so that it foreshortens greatly the task of understanding *Hamlet* as an example of drama and demonstrates the play's worth and scope with remarkable economy. It also, by having the mirror that is art reflect itself instead of nature, seems to enclose and intensify what is going on. If theater itself can become Hamlet's means to his end, or even if it is only his excuse for delay, then differences between the mirror and nature tend to be erased and the mimesis is, by a kind of sleight-of-hand, even more effective. We feel that we get closer to reality as the art–reality distinction disintegrates.

In that respect, one ought to be able to predict, just from glancing at Hamlet's advice out of context, that nature, as the play portrays it, will itself seem to be full of mirrors; that life, beyond the players and their performance, will itself begin to grow theatrical and illusory; that roles and acting and arranged scenarios will come to be characteristic of the play's action at every turn. The spread of theatricality follows logically from the dissolving of the distinction between life and theater, but it takes a playwright of genius to pursue the implications of that logic as fully as Shakespeare pursues them in *Hamlet*.

When Hamlet has finished his advice to the players he turns to Horatio. Their joint purpose, it turns out, will be to watch not the play but the king, "in censure of his seeming." The point is to study the deficiencies in Claudius's acting. As the court approaches, Hamlet slips into his own part with the comment, "I must be idle." The point is to keep his own acting consistent. And so it goes. This is not the place to document the theatricality of *Hamlet* in detail. Alert readers will already have glimpsed its pervasiveness. As the boundary between the players and their world, on the one hand, and the larger world of the play, on the other, begins to break down, a fundamental unity is established that not only binds the disparate elements together more tightly but also argues for art's effectiveness by making it both a means to an end and an end in itself, about the world and about itself at the same time, with no difficulties ensuing from that apparent division of interest. Nothing fails more emphatically than self-reflexive art that falls into incestuous self-regard, preciousness, and narcissism. By the same token, perhaps nothing succeeds more emphatically than a self-reflexive art whose consciousness of its own scope, function, and limits feels liberating rather than limiting. Self-referential art had a large future when Shakespeare used the players and the play in *Hamlet*; its past was sketchy at best.

Making use of the players, once he has introduced them, for a number of different purposes and in two different acts is an example of the final type of thrift one can find Shakespeare employing in *Hamlet*. It might be called *intrastructural thrift*, since it involves the reuse of elements that either might well have been used only once or with which reemployment takes a very unusual form.

As with the other cases of recycled structure, the purpose of such recursion seems not so much frugality as enhanced meaning. Folklorists and anthropologists, as I noted earlier, use terms like *embedding* and *nesting* to characterize the intensifying of meaning through calculated structures of repetition, variation, and replication. Literary criticism has in the past tended to use metaphoric terms like *mirroring* and *echoing*. Whatever we choose to term the phenomenon, its extensive presence in *Hamlet* has long been recognized. The proliferation of father-and-son relationships is a good example. It is an elaboration that achieves economy by means of repetition. As opportunities to compare the situations of Fortinbras and Laertes with that of Hamlet confront us, we realize that they all confer meaning upon each other in an extremely efficient way. If we remember that Pyrrhus, in the speech the player dredges up for Hamlet, is also an avenging son, we find we can add to the galaxy (or nest) of such characters and glimpse meanings in Hamlet's choice and in the contrast between hellish Pyrrhus and thoughtful Hamlet that are sharply enhanced by all the other parallels.

Parallelism among characters even becomes something of a joke when their interchangeability is stressed. Rosencrantz and Guildenstern are the most notable example of this, of course, but they seem to have their own parallels in Cornelius and Voltemand, and possibly in Marcellus and Barnardo. In a different vein, as I suggested earlier, Osric strikes us as a kind of duplicate of, or replacement for, Polonius. Osric is of course more foolish and less meddlesome, but the difference in age is enough to account for that; he simply needs seasoning to turn into Polonius. And while time becomes a factor through that recognition and by virtue of the succession of these two characters, we come away from the Hamlet-Osric encounter not only remembering Hamlet-Polonius encounters but also feeling that a man like Hamlet would always find such people in a court to practice his wit upon. The recognition gives a kind of timelessness to the exchanges as well.

Recurring situations also abound in *Hamlet,* and most of them are quite well known. The fact that the dilations could be schematized into four categories is one evidence of this patterning. So are events that precede the opening of the play and then recur within it, such as the ghost's visits to the platform and Claudius's habit of turning to poison as an instrument of murder. Instances of spying and overhearing are so common that it scarcely surprises us when Polonius moves so promptly from the conclusion of one—listening in with Claudius to Hamlet's interview with Ophelia—to the engineering of the next, Hamlet's visit to Gertrude's closet. Their frequency makes Hamlet's own fourth-act comment, "How all occasions do inform against me," plausible in turn, though he is applying it more to the way he is often provoked to self-accusatory soliloquies than to the proliferation of informers and spying.

One of the lost aspects of Shakespeare's original staging of *Hamlet* about which we can only conjecture is the use of visual parallelisms. Just as we do not know enough about the *Ur-Hamlet* to delineate the relationships between the two plays in any detail, so we are reduced to guessing about which aspects of performance originally achieved intrastructural economies through visual parallels. A few interesting possibilities present themselves, however. The discovery space, the area at the back of the stage that could be closed off, was often used to frame and isolate characters at special moments and in special situations. It seems the likely place, for example, for Ophelia to retire to pray or read while Hamlet delivers his "To be or not to be" soliloquy in act 3. There she could be visible but conventionally out of earshot. It is also the likely place for Claudius to be praying when Hamlet comes upon him after the play-within-the-play. If both Claudius and Ophelia pray there, then, we have a striking parallel present in performance but not indicated in the text.[14]

On the other hand, that same discovery space with its curtain drawn is the possible place of concealment for Claudius and Polonius in the "nunnery" scene (in which case Ophelia must be placed on the stage proper), and if that is the case we have a strong link with the arras through which Hamlet will stab Polonius a few scenes later. If the space is identical to the one Claudius himself used earlier to spy on Hamlet, the "rashness" of Hamlet's act is mitigated by the curious logic of performance. We cannot have all of these parallels involving the discovery space—either Ophelia is back there and Claudius and Polonius are offstage or they are there and she is on the main stage—but that some of them were operative in performance seems unquestionable, and they thus take their place among the structural economies Shakespeare employs in *Hamlet,* mirrorings of different events within the action.

While it is possible that the ghost came and went through the discovery space, I am more inclined to feel that he used the trap, at least for some of his entrances and exits. That makes the "fellow in the cellarage" joke more germane and underlines the ghost's ontological ambiguity, since the understage area, known as "hell," was the familiar place from which devils came and went in the morality and miracle plays.[15] What makes that lost visual emphasis especially stunning here, however, is the fifth-act use of the trap for the gravediggers and for Ophelia's burial. The two uses of the understage area, accessible by trapdoor, in effect bracket the play's action. What began as a mysterious and thrilling region where spirits came and went and a father's ghost spoke, demanding revenge, has turned into a place in which death means physical dissolution— skulls and bones and jokes about how long corpses last in the earth, and who builds till Doomsday, and what might have become of the valiant dust of Alexander the Great (another son fulfilling the destiny shaped by his father). Here the parallels help us understand all sorts of connections between father and son, old play and new play, and the progression Hamlet has made toward an understanding of death that holds the mirror up not so much to the supernatural— ghosts and metaphysical speculations—as to nature, especially the unpleasant smell of an old skull. Yorick, dead but still somehow a spiritual presence, emerges from the grave to "instruct" Hamlet, as a kind of foster father, in a detachment toward life that takes death's terrors and mysteries away. The reuse of graves—Yorick and some anonymous companions are being dug up to make room for Ophelia—was an imaginative preoccupation for Shakespeare's generation, as poems by Donne and Shakespeare's own epitaph remind us.[16] The economy was necessitated by the limited amount of sacred ground available, but whatever its origins it strikes us, in this context, as a kind of emblem for the fantastic thrift of *Hamlet*. That the space the ghost disappeared into could ultimately be the same one where jokes about death, as well as Yorick's reappearance, Ophelia's burial, and Hamlet's first of two struggles with Laertes could occur, is simply something we could never have predicted in the first act. An old tradition says that the playwright himself acted the ghost; what fun to think of him then doubling later on as the grave-digger! Certainly the double-casting that was necessary in Shakespeare's company—which probably, for instance, involved having Osric resemble Polonius partly so that the same actor could play-fully play with their kinship and kindness, likeness and difference, while playing both—is yet another example of how reuse, or nesting, or whatever we may choose to call it, looms so large in the design of *Hamlet.* Such notions give us a measure of how far the play has come, as well as of the economy of means by which the theater has made that distance possible. If there had been no trap-door leading to a hell space under the stage in Shakespeare's theater, he might well have had to invent it for *Hamlet.* But the point, of course, is that it was already there. With characteristic thrift Shakespeare was employing something completely familiar for a purpose that felt astonishingly new. The practice is so typical of *Hamlet* and of Shakespeare's art in general, that it is easy to take for granted and easy to overlook.

Having *Hamlet* before us makes it hard to imagine alternatives, but we need to do that as a way of closing this consideration. Imagine a play that combines an endlessly elaborating and inventive verbal impulse with a comparable desire for novelty and complication in its plot design. Examples like *Cymbeline* and *Peer Gynt* come to mind. Then imagine a play that recycles a familiar story and practices economies based on repetition and reflexivity while also pursuing a deliberately concentrated and recursive style. One thinks of plays by writers like Beckett and Pinter. Such plays might feel more consistent within themselves because they match their uses of language to their dramatic constructions, but they don't sound more appealing than *Hamlet.* That seems to be the point. Dilatory style, on the one hand, and thrifty structure, on the other, served Shakespeare so well in this instance that they feel inevitable. We may take their partnership for granted until we step back to recognize that Shakespeare the gifted poet and Shakespeare the richly experienced man of the theater could not have divided and then reunited himself in this way without a deliberate effort at innovation.

Chapter Two

Storytelling
and Complicity
in *Othello*

We all marvel at *Hamlet*'s complexity and the impossibility of ever doing it full justice in performance or by way of interpretation, but the fact remains that *Hamlet* is great fun, both in the theater, where it almost never fails to thrill, move, and entertain, and in the study and the classroom, where it seems to inspire us to some of our best insights and observations. *Othello*, which most people take to be a simpler play, is finally a good deal more troubling. Statistics are not kept, so far as I know, on which of Shakespeare's plays is hardest to bring off in performance. The difficulty quotient no doubt varies; we used to think the problem comedies notoriously hard to produce, but in recent years they have had a vogue which has shown them to be eminently playable, stimulating for actors and audiences alike. Something comparable has occurred with the late romances. Despite such variations, I suspect that *Othello* has proved consistently more difficult to produce successfully, at least in our century, than almost any other Shakespeare play. I have yet to see a successful production, and I can count the ones that have had the reputation of success on the fingers of one hand. The tragedies are never easy to bring off; they ask a great deal of their actors and, of course, their audiences. But *Othello*'s difficulties exceed, I think, even those of *Hamlet, Lear, Macbeth,* or the Roman tragedies.

Why should this be so? Some might say it is the racial question, dogging this play the way the vexed question of anti-Semitism has dogged *The Merchant of Venice.* No doubt that has played a part, but I think that the fundamental difficulty of *Othello* goes deeper, and that it has beset the criticism of the play from the beginning (for example, in Thomas Rymer) as consistently as it has the productions. It has to do with the jeopardizing of our regard for the tragic hero and our temptation to affiliate ourselves emotionally and philosophically with the villain. If *Othello* is a tragedy, it is one that is very delicately balanced, sailing close to the wind in risking our skepticism about its hero's right to our sympathy and respect. You can argue that Shakespeare was unaware of the risk he was taking and that the problem of our sympathy has developed over time as a result of our changing attitudes toward love, adultery, soldiers, Moors, and sexual jealousy. My own inclination is to see Shakespeare as perfectly conscious of the risk he had in hand and indeed delighting in its challenge. Such an approach, I would maintain, is far more likely than the others to do justice to a play over which even such redoubtable interpreters as T. S. Eliot and Robert B. Heilman get thrown off course by the almost fatal attraction of Iago's viewpoint.

To come at the play's design and meaning in a way that avoids the pitfalls that so many commentators—not to mention directors and actors—have tumbled into, I think it is necessary to move beyond simple character analysis. It is not just a matter of fully understanding Othello's psyche, or, even more to the point, Iago's. We must understand how they are counterposed to each other through choices made about the play's style, or styles, and how the risk I have said Shakespeare is consciously taking is in great part a matter of how he chooses to handle dramatic structure. To be even more specific: we cannot vindicate Othello without a proper understanding of style, and we cannot keep Iago in his place and free ourselves from his treachery without a full understanding of structure. Those are the twin tasks that lie ahead of us in this chapter.

A ROUND UNVARNISH'D TALE

If narrative was one of four discursive possibilities in *Hamlet,* it emerges in *Othello* as a major impulse and a leading stylistic feature. We know that this play is partly a war of styles or rhetorics, each based on a different view of human nature and of human love; we may not have noticed how much Othello's mode derives from his gift for storytelling, a gift that Iago deftly usurps for his own purposes and that Othello briefly recovers at the play's close, in partial redemption from the terrible fall we have witnessed. My contention is that the passing of the storyteller's art from Othello to Iago and back again is a stylistic configuration that outlines one of the play's curves of action and meaning. I shall try to sketch out the evidence on which this thesis rests.

We might begin by asking why narrative was chosen as the significant expression of Othello's heroism. For one thing, it seems to link him to the worlds of romance and epic, where narrative was, for Shakespeare and his audience, the natural medium. The associations with romance suggest a life of mysterious adventures in which inexplicable vicissitudes alternate with miraculous escapes and rescues. The associations with epic call up the exploits of military heroism against a background of momentous historical events. Both links lend interest and dignity to this exotic stranger—"extravagant and wheeling," as Roderigo calls him in act 1, scene 1— who has moved about in the very locales where romances and epics were traditionally set.

We also come to realize that Othello, as a way of orienting himself in Venice and as a means of bringing order to the rich chaos of his world and experience, has come to trust narrative as a natural organizing principle. This would help explain why he relies on patterned and ceremonious narratives while Iago, his antagonist, reveals an ominous ability to improvise.

The very first narratives of the play are in fact Iago's, and they are not notable for coherence or effectiveness. Telling Roderigo the story of his denied promotion, Iago falls into exaggeration ("three great ones of the city") and is given to little digressions about himself and Othello and, at greater length, Cassio. He gets the necessary information across, but not in a way that makes us sit back and admire his poise as a narrator or the smooth progression of his tale. We find him in mid-story again as the second scene opens, trying to stir Othello up with a phony anecdote about someone who prated against the Moor in "scurvy and provoking terms." His listener does not react with the anger that the story expresses and hopes to arouse. On the basis of the play's opening scenes we might rate Iago a competent purveyor of racial slurs and sexual epithets, but we would have to give him low marks as a storyteller; he is too given to interruption, digression, and exaggeration to reach an audience smarter than Roderigo. Shakespeare hasn't helped Iago's case by twice bringing him on in mid-narrative, as if his rambling stories were not worth bothering about in their entirety. We don't know how he starts his tales, but we can see that they tend to flow roughly and finish lamely.

If Iago could be said to need some lessons in the art of narrative, he has ample opportunity from the master he follows in order "to serve a turn" upon. In a grand setting, and to a notable audience, Othello tells the story of his love, which is in turn an account of how his storytelling won him a bride he might never have expected to even look his way. The story, then, is double—the story of a love and the story of a life—and it constitutes both internal (by its content) and external (by its telling) evidence of the validity of Othello's marriage, a validity that is then confirmed by Desdemona's entrance and her own testimony.[1]

There are a number of fundamental excellences in this master performance. The preliminary statement contains a complimentary address to the audience; a factual admission of the charge, or part of it; an apologia; and a promise that creates audience, occasion, and a sense of expectation:

> Most potent, grave, and reverend signiors,
> My very noble and approv'd good masters;
> That I have ta'en away this old man's daughter,
> It is most true: true, I have married her,
> The very head and front of my offending
> Hath this extent, no more. Rude am I in my speech,
> And little blest with the set phrase of peace,
> For since these arms of mine had seven years' pith,
> Till now some nine moons wasted, they have us'd
> Their dearest action in the tented field,
> And little of this great world can I speak,
> More than pertains to feats of broil, and battle,
> And therefore little shall I grace my cause,
> In speaking for myself: yet, (by your gracious patience)
> I will a round unvarnish'd tale deliver,
> Of my whole course of love, what drugs, what charms,
> What conjuration, and what mighty magic,
> (For such proceedings am I charged withal)
> I won his daughter.
>
> [1.3.76–94][2]

This deft prologue serves the purpose of deflecting Brabantio's charges, and it survives an interruption from that quarter, giving Othello the floor and everyone's undivided attention. It is a useful technique for anyone who wants to tell a tale without interruption and on a ground that has been cleared to facilitate its telling, and Iago, as we will see, takes note of it. At the same time, Desdemona is sent for, creating a curious, almost magical sense that if the story is successful it will conjure its subject to appear in flesh and blood, an effect for which there are interesting parallels: we noted one in the discussion of the opening of *Hamlet,* and we will see many other "magical entrances" in our explorations of *King Lear* and *Macbeth*.[3] The fact that Iago is sent to fetch Desdemona, and by doing so misses the main part of the story, might seem to suggest that he cannot benefit from Othello's example in the way I have suggested, but by the curious logic of stage performance, his participation in the bringing of Desdemona gives him an intimacy with the story at least as great as if he had stood by listening to it.

Othello begins by noting his accuser's partial responsibility for the outcome of the tale. The auditor who first loved Othello for the way he could tell the story of his life was not Desdemona but her father:

> Her father lov'd me, oft invited me,
> Still question'd me the story of my life,
> From year to year; the battles, sieges, fortunes,
> That I have pass'd:
> I ran it through, even from my boyish days,
> To the very moment that he bade me tell it.
>
> [1.3.128–33]

If, as commentators have suggested, there is such a thing as "double time" in this play it could be said to begin here, for Othello must handle two separate time frames: that one, involving his courtship, with which he begins and ends, and, inside it, the older and longer one of his life "even from my boyish days / To the very moment that he bade me tell it." These two time schemes are so smoothly managed that they tend to merge, giving greater validity to the story as a whole and making the courtship seem an inevitable part of the life. The temporal process that has brought Othello to this moment has involved a threefold sequence: (1) he suffered vicissitudes and saw marvels; (2) he learned to translate these experiences into language, becoming such a powerful recounter of them that he engrossed first Brabantio and then Desdemona; (3) Desdemona's desire to hear the tale in its entirety led to their intimacy and mutual sympathy. She saw his "visage in his mind"—her vision transcending his external appearance—or, as he puts it, she loved him for the dangers he had passed, *through* his ability to recount them powerfully, and he loved her that she did pity them, responding so fully both to the experiences and to the ability to recreate them. Othello's richly detailed and vibrantly musical account to the Senate really runs this sequence backward and then forward, so that it both partakes of time and transcends it, a feature that the finest narratives often seem to possess.

The "traveller's history" (I favor the Folio reading here over Quarto's "travel's history") that Othello has often recounted is full of dubious but fascinating details. It has rescues, accidents, enslavements, and escapes, spectacular scenery (notable especially for dryness and desolation), and the cannibals and headless men who were shorthand in Shakespeare's day for tall tales and stretched beliefs. Because Othello merely glances at such details as incidental to his main narrative—a domestic tale that was enacted in Brabantio's sitting rooms—he cannot stand accused of exploiting our taste for the exotic, even though our glimpses of the "dilated pilgrimage" allow us a vicarious thrill or two. The tension between the exotic life story and the domestic story framing it, like the fusing of the time frames and the judicious prologue, show Othello to be a master storyteller without implying that he is hypocritical or manipulative. He emerges looking splendid.

The Duke's validation of what we have heard—"I think this tale would win my daughter too"—may especially commend the tale within the tale, but it does not distinguish it from the entire story. Nor does it address matters of truth or fiction, right or wrong. It simply acknowledges the power of story and storyteller a moment before Desdemona confirms the truth and accuracy of Othello's account, along with the reciprocity—she was "half the wooer too"—of their love. The tale wins on both counts: as a *true* story and as a *good* story—and Othello's victory is complete.

But the stage clears, to show us a very thoughtful Iago, so bemused by what he has seen and heard that Roderigo has trouble getting his attention. He has entered at the concluding of Othello's tale and has witnessed its effect on the audience. We usually take his abstraction here to suggest his pondering of devices and practices, but I would add, on the basis of his later behavior, that he's considering the power and importance of good storytelling. As the play proceeds, he will become a better and better narrator, while Othello's gift for storytelling will decline until the closing moments, when Iago chooses silence and Othello tells a last tale that, once more, merges strangely and powerfully with reality. Until that moment, Desdemona's cue—"if I had a friend that lov'd her, / I should but teach him how to tell my story"—is monstrously perverted by Othello's thoughtful ensign, who learns to tell not his captain's story but some powerful stories of his own.

In act 2, scene 3, when pressed by Othello and others to explain the brawl that has roused the "snorting citizens" and brought Othello to the verge of violent rage, Iago gets his first big chance to use the storytelling art effectively. Like Othello in the first act, he waits for the situation to create a strong need for a tale that will resolve a mystery. He then uses a prologue, just as Othello did in act 1, managing to implicate Cassio before the story is even told:

> I had rather ha' this tongue cut from my mouth,
> Than it should do offense to Michael Cassio:
> Yet I persuade myself, to speak the truth
> Shall nothing wrong him. Thus it is, general

[2.3.212–15]

The modest little report that follows produces exactly the reaction from Othello that Iago intends—"I know, Iago, / Thy honesty and love doth mince this matter, / Making it light to Cassio"—and its judicious use of detail (for instance, "I heard the clink and fall of swords; / And Cassio high in oaths") and of generalizations ("But men are men; the best sometimes forget") shows a sense of occasion and of the power of narrative to order, summarize, and control experience that begins to rival the mastery Othello demonstrated in the first act. What especially impresses us, I think, is that Iago succeeds in having Cassio dismissed, while telling a story that nobody challenges or repudiates. Iago has made sure his tale is true and that its witnesses are present to confirm it. This duplication of the validation of Othello's speech in act 1 by truthful narrative and the corroboration of witnesses gives Iago and Othello a special bond in terms of the play's rhetorical patterns that will help make their late partnership, and especially Othello's great trust, the more plausible.

Iago's next move will be to ask for a further detail from the grand story of the first act: "Did Michael Cassio, when you woo'd my lady, / Know of your love?" (3.3.95–96). The implication is that an important fact may have been overlooked, that the story was an imperfect account. The same effect is achieved by Iago's adding a detail of his own to the original account a moment later: "She did deceive her father, marrying you; / And when she seem'd to shake and fear your looks, / She loved them most" (3.3.210–12). Othello assents to this, and it's as though these small emendations of his original narrative were both altering the reality he attempted to represent and undermining his authority as a storyteller.

Iago's next tale, and his most crucial piece of storytelling in the play, is his response to Othello's demand for "a living reason she's disloyal" (again, I prefer the Folio reading to the Quarto's "a living reason that she's disloyal"). The word "living" is curious here, and if its main sense is "sound" or "valid," it has a way of referring us to the power of narrative to recreate experience in a convincing way. The tale that answers this demand, while totally untrue, has the vividness, the "living" quality, that we associate with effective narratives; we can discern the difference between the two connotations even while Othello, not surprisingly, confuses liveliness with honesty, good story with true story, and is taken in.

Iago again uses the device of prologue:

I do not like the office,
But sith I am enter'd into this cause so far,
Prick'd to 't by foolish honesty and love,
I will go on.

[3.3.416–19]

This is the same preliminary resistance he displayed in act 2, and it deftly echoes Othello's own "Rude am I in my speech," so that a double reminder of Iago's demonstrated honesty, and of his shared role with Othello as a modest relater of events that resolve mysteries, is accomplished before he even begins his tale.

"I lay with Cassio lately" again involves us in the famous "double time" that has fretted the commentators. In that respect it is a flagrant and unsettling opening (not unlike saying, "Her father loved me"!), followed immediately by the intriguing matter of the raging tooth and the sleeplessness. Hamlet's sleeplessness rose from a kind of fighting in his heart, but in Iago's emphatically physical world a toothache is a better excuse, and even a soul like a tooth, is capable of being loosened and can allow leaks of private thoughts and sexual disclosures:

> There are a kind of men so loose of soul,
> That in their sleeps will mutter their affairs,
> One of this kind is Cassio.
>
> [3.3.422–24]

This skillful transition, with its generalization that will go off in a moment like a depth charge, sets up an especially vivid piece of narrative. Iago might have claimed merely to have overheard Cassio's muttering; instead he claims to have experienced at first hand a version of the guilty lovers' physical passion:

> In sleep I heard him say "Sweet Desdemona,
> Let us be wary, let us hide our loves;"
> And then, sir, would he gripe and wring my hand,
> Cry out, "Sweet creature!" and then kiss me hard,
> As if he pluck'd up kisses by the roots,
> That grew upon my lips, then laid his leg
> Over my thigh, and sigh'd, and kiss'd, and then
> Cried "Cursed fate, that gave thee to the Moor!"
>
> [3.3.425–32]

Iago can now contend that this was only a dream because he has established the theory about loose-souled men who mutter their affairs. A moment later he nails the matter home with a piece of narrative so brief and so effective that it takes our breath away:

> I know not that, but such a handkerchief—
> I am sure it was your wife's—did I to-day
> See Cassio wipe his beard with.
>
> [3.3.443–45]

The boldness, economy, and vividness of Iago's narrative here go a long way toward insuring the success of his practice on Othello. The thinly disguised sexual implication—wiping a beard is bound to suggest a postcoital cleanup on some level of consciousness— and the implied contempt for Desdemona that the alleged action shows achieve precisely what Iago needs: an apparently innocent action masks suggestions that will "burn like the mines of sulphur" in poor Othello's blood. In the first scene of act 4 Iago takes matters a step further by reporting that Cassio has told him the story of the affair and that while Othello watches from a distance and does "but mark his gesture," Iago "will make him tell the tale anew." Othello's willingness to accept Iago's word for the content of a tale he watches in pantomime marks the degree of his deterioration and of Iago's increasing control over him.

A comparable indication of Othello's degradation is what happens to his own storytelling powers, as suggested by the tale he tells Desdemona about the handkerchief. Compare the speech rhythms and control of sequence in this narrative to those in the tale he told in the first act:

> That handkerchief
> Did an Egyptian to my mother give,
> She was a charmer, and could almost read
> The thoughts of people; she told her, while she
>   kept it
> 'Twould make her amiable, and subdue my father
> Entirely to her love: but if she lost it,
> Or made a gift of it, my father's eye

Should hold her loathly, and his spirits should hunt
After new fancies: she dying, gave it me,
And bid me, when my fate would have me wive,
To give it her; I did so, and take heed on't,
Make it a darling, like your precious eye,
To lose, or give't away, were such perdition
As nothing else could match.

[3.4.53–66]

We're very conscious of the degree of invention that lies behind this jerky and presumably improvised story. Desdemona's reaction—"Is 't possible?"—would seem to be the right one, but it produces a further segment of the tale that is even more preposterous:

'Tis true, there's magic in the web of it;
A sibyl, that had number'd in the world
The sun to make two hundred compasses,
In her prophetic fury sew'd the work;
The worms were hallow'd that did breed the silk,
And it was dyed in mummy, which the skillful
Conserve of maidens' hearts.

[67–73]

Again, Desdemona's reaction is not the delight she presumably first experienced on hearing Othello's tales, but the issue of veracity: "I' faith! Is 't true?" I think this tale would make my daughter question too! Other commentators have remarked on the disrupted syntax and disjointed thinking here, but not on the perversion of the narrative capability Othello showed so clearly in the first act. The "time transcendence" that I posited as characteristic of the greatest narratives and impressively present in Othello's courtship narrative, is invoked this time in a kind of parodic form, as represented by mummification and the sibyl's lifespan; it hardly needs pointing out that this is far less satisfactory and more forced than it was in the first act. The occasion has such a different tone that, while we can recognize that the story and its details reflect Othello's demonstrated storytelling powers, we should mainly be aware of the falling-off between his first great story and this overblown travesty of its form and style.

I pass by some other interesting examples of narrative—Desdemona's tale of Barbary; or the broken and incoherent narratives that Othello offers Desdemona just before he kills her, for instance; as well as other examples of Iago's narrative skills—in order to move to a consideration of Othello's recovery of narrative powers at the close of the play. There are many reasons for Iago's announced intention to remain silent in the denouement, all of them compelling, but one of them is surely the practical matter of returning the center of attention to Othello, giving him the floor, so to speak. Othello uses the opportunity once again to command the rapt attention of an audience and demonstrate his ability to narrate powerfully. He actually instructs his listeners in how they ought to tell his story—"When you shall these unlucky deeds relate"—and gives them a compelling narrative analogue, the base Indian and the priceless pearl, for the events they must try to understand. He turns then to narrative itself, the story of his encounter with the Turk and Venetian in Aleppo. Since the handkerchief story may have been invented for its occasion, this one might well come under the same suspicion were it not for the fact that Othello deflects questions of its authenticity by making it another narrative analogue to the story we have been watching, exposing its true purpose and moving its action to the level of immediate reality. "O bloody period!" says Lodovico, embodying our recognitions in one of those astonishing Shakespearean puns—in this case on duration, completion, syntax, and a punctuation mark (the menses association is apparently a much later one)—that seem to crop up at such moments. The turning of the Aleppo story into the stage-reality of Othello's death, its reification, is comparable to the appearance of Desdemona in act 1 and her confirmation of the truth of the first great story. It should serve to remind us that Othello at his best had powers of invention and expression which, while set at the outer limits of belief, had a factual kinship with the reality of the play that made them ideal and wholly successful.[4]

All of Shakespeare's tragic heroes possess some type of imaginative superiority to the world around them. Othello's is manifested in his storytelling gift, and there is nothing evasive about his resort to metaphor—that is, to the Indian (or Judean) and pearl that so distressed another poet, Eliot, who should have known better than to be literal-minded about figurative speech. There is every indication that Shakespeare meant, by having Othello recover his heroic and even spiritual power to tell a story and hold an audience, to show us that he had recognized his error and to that extent regained the nobility and mastery from which he had been deflected, in part by the very skills of language and storytelling he prided himself on. Othello regains control and command of his life story by telling it once more, one vivid portion of it, and by exercising his power to end it—story and life and finally even the play we are watching. He becomes here not only the soldier who recognizes his responsibility to his own fate, a restoration of self and integrity we had desperately wished he would come to sooner, but the maker or fabricator who recognizes his responsibility to tell a good story and give it an appropriate ending: "no way but this, / Killing myself, to die upon a kiss." Here again, as in the great first-act narrative and, parodically, in the story of the handkerchief's creation, we have a kind of transcendence of normal time. The anecdote about something that happened "in Aleppo once" and the hero's long and colorful life story, often told but never truly concluded till this moment, converge with the tragedy itself like lines that did not seem to have a common intersection until an act of will and creative skill gave them this bloody period, this point. The convergence greatly strengthens our sense of the play's and Othello's combined abilities to finish in a just and timely way.

Let me emphasize that I have not simply been talking about a rhetorical skill. It is of course the *content* of Othello's stories that brings his values to life for us. The same is true of Iago's stories. But we do not distinguish between form and content, narrative skill and narrative authenticity, while watching the play. Nor are we meant to brood about distinctions between literal fact and fictive invention. One should not worry about whether Othello really smote a Turk in Aleppo or invented the incident as a means to a heroic expurgation of his guilt and anguish. The medium validates the message, and vice versa. As the hero's storytelling powers wax and wane, so does our sense of his goodness and heroism. If we try to separate style from substance at the play's conclusion, as critics like Leavis and Eliot have done, we miss the point of Shakespeare's overall design.

IAGO AND OUR COMPLICITY

If the question of who is the best storyteller, according to the criteria outlined in the first part of this chapter, were the primary issue of *Othello,* then we should have little or no trouble in determining that our sympathies lie with Othello and against the jeopardizing of his validity as warrior, lover, and narrator by Iago. But the experience of the play, as anyone familiar with the body of commentary on it can testify, is a good deal more complicated. There is a countertendency at work in the experiencing of Othello as hero and Iago as villain, something equivalent to the tension between stylistic dilation and structural thrift in *Hamlet.*

We are used to seeing *Othello* as a war of verbal styles; but the larger problem with Iago is that of our peculiar relationship with him, and that is in fact a structural device. When a dramatic character speaks directly to us, through aside or soliloquy or direct address, a special relationship is created. The effect is comparable to the use of first-person narrative in fiction (or to the kind of third-person narrative that concentrates on the consciousness of a central character); the sharing of perspective creates an automatic sympathy, a bond of common knowledge, and a point from which to view the other characters and the action. Indeed, it could be argued that this effect is even more powerful on the stage because of the physical interaction that occurs between live actor and live audience, though it is also, because less frequently used, ordinarily more diffuse. Confiding in us what is not said to other characters on stage, whether it be through direct discourse or privileged overhearing, will not let a character altogether escape criticism or judgment, of course. Still, our sense of having seen things from the character's point of view will color any judgment or criticism; such opinions will be more self-conscious, more thoughtfully rendered, and will somewhat resemble self-criticism or self-condemnation.

The use of this effect and its various possibilities is everywhere evident in Shakespeare, not least as a means of balancing preference and distributing sympathy. Isn't the taunting and hoaxing of Malvolio, along with his ultimate angry exit from *Twelfth Night,* more difficult to accept because the man, however ridiculous or wrongheaded he may be, has admitted us to some of his most intimate thoughts and feelings? Knowing what it is like to be Malvolio— Shylock is another such example—we are at times nonplussed by the insensitivity and contempt of the other characters. They are right about him, of course, but not from his point of view, and insofar as we have entered that point of view, we will be divided between their attitude and his. In *Measure for Measure* we would naturally like to side with the benevolent Duke, who manipulates the action, while despising the priggish and corrupted Angelo; but the fact that the Duke confides in us so little and that Angelo is honest with himself, and thus with us, about the details of his inner life, the experience of a mind and imagination overwhelmed by desire, realigns our sympathies somewhat and makes the play more problematic to interpret, more complex to experience, more *measured.*

For many, *Othello* has been the most painful of Shakespeare's tragedies to watch or read.[5] *Lear* is, of course, full of suffering and cruelty, and no one experiences that play with equanimity, but a particular dread accompanies the movement into the third, fourth, and fifth acts of *Othello,* that period from the Moor's first temptation through to Desdemona's murder. I think it is no accident that *Othello* tends to be cited as the primary example of a play in which members of the audience might forget themselves and interrupt a performance in order to warn the other characters about Iago. In a well-known consideration of aesthetic distance, Edward Bullough, for example, wondered whether a jealous man would be unfit to appreciate *Othello* because of the way he would confuse Othello's situation with his own.[6] But a jealous man is no more likely to lose his sense of aesthetic distance during *Othello* than anyone else. If members of the audience forget they are at a play or find their own enforced silence unbearable, it will not be because they suffer from jealousy but because they wish to prevent the murder of Desdemona and expose the villainy of Iago.

The choice of this play for that kind of example is, I think, most telling. It acknowledges how painful it is to be silent witness to the action of *Othello*. That pain is in great part based on Shakespeare's extensive use of the confiding principle. The sharing of Iago's perspective through aside, soliloquy, and direct address to the audience makes us his uneasy and unwilling accomplices, a Shakespearean dramatic experiment that is both exciting and risky. Making a villain who deserves no sympathy the character whose point of view we share most fully is skating on very thin ice. It endangers the whole enterprise of tragedy, and the problematic result is evident in *Othello* criticism, where the problem of seeing the play and its hero so extensively through the eyes of Iago creates endless differences among the commentators.[7]

Act I can be seen as delineating the first of Iago's plots, the practice of his mischief, but we see it in these terms because of the way he confides his feelings and purposes to Roderigo; he will not begin to take us directly into his confidence until the end of the act, so that our relation to him through the course of the exposition is a relatively easy one, with our problematic complicity yet to be established.

The first act, as is often noted, is almost a play unto itself, in which Iago tries and fails to disrupt Othello's marriage and discredit him on his wedding night.[8] The plot is foiled by Othello's self-possession and by the eloquence, discussed earlier, with which he recounts how he and Desdemona fell in love. His "round unvar-nish'd tale," delivered in public and with emphasis on candor and openness, is the opposite of Iago's confidential and secretive speech—to himself, to us, to Roderigo, and later to Cassio and Othello. Even as Othello dissociates himself from secrecy and from confidences, Iago is preparing to make such utterances the basis of his peculiar relationship with us. As the Senate meeting breaks up in plans to repel the Turks and fortify Cyprus, we find Iago and Roderigo alone together, the one manipulating the other in a man-ner now familiar from the play's opening, so that Iago's language of deception stands as a frame around Othello's—and Desde-mona's—language of candor, his guile existing before and after their openness. This is ominous enough. But as Roderigo leaves and Iago himself might be expected to exit, he turns instead and begins to address us directly, establishing a new kind of relationship with us and sharing with us his pleasure in his own cleverness and skill. Our first reaction may well be amusement and delight, though as the speech advances our attitude should begin to change:

> Thus do I ever make my fool my purse:
> For I mine own gain'd knowledge should profane,
> If I would time expend with such a snipe
> But for my sport and profit: I hate the Moor,
> And it is thought abroad, that 'twixt my sheets
> He's done my office; I know not if't be true . . .
> Yet I, for mere suspicion in that kind,
> Will do, as if for surety: he holds me well,
> The better shall my purpose work on him.
> Cassio's a proper man, let me see now,
> To get this place, and to make up my will,
> A double knavery . . . how, how? . . . let me see,
> After some time, to abuse Othello's ear,
> That he is too familiar with his wife:
> He hath a person and a smooth dispose,
> To be suspected, fram'd to make women false:

The Moor a free and open nature too,
That thinks men honest that but seems to be so:
And will as tenderly be led by the nose . . .
As asses are.
I ha't, it is engender'd; Hell and night
Must bring this monstrous birth to the world's light.

[1.3.381–402]

There is something specious about this confiding, but we aren't in any position to recognize that at this point. What mainly impresses us is that Iago, the deceiver, has a candor of his own; he has given us a special perspective, a privileged vantage point, from which to watch the ensuing action. Even if he never addressed another word directly to us, we would have a great deal to go on in interpreting his actions through the rest of the play.

But of course he does, to our growing distress, address us again. And again. In act 2, scene 1, he resumes the relationship with an easy familiarity, a sort of chummy assumption that we are willing accomplices. Watching Cassio and Desdemona together, he positions himself close to the audience (that blocking would seem to be demanded by the text) so that he can comment on his own attitudes and intentions. His speech is usually marked (*aside*) to indicate that it is intended only for the audience while there are other characters present, but it is rather extended for an aside. Desdemona, for example, has a more typical aside in the same scene:

I am not merry; but I do beguile
The thing I am by seeming otherwise.

[2.1.122–23]

This sort of brief glimpse into the character's feelings is intended as a kind of correcting of our impression, in the same way that characters may reassure us from behind disguises, as, for example, Edgar does in *King Lear*. Iago's aside is of a different length and character:

He takes her by the palm; ay, well said, whisper: as little a web as this will ensnare as great a fly as Cassio. Ay, smile upon her, do: I will catch you in your own courtesies: you say true, 'tis so indeed. If such tricks as these strip you out of your lieutenantry, it had been better you had not kiss'd your three fingers so oft, which now again you are most apt to play the sir in: good, well kiss'd, an excellent courtesy; 'tis so, indeed: yet again, your fingers at your lips? would they were clyster-pipes for your sake ... [2.1.167–77]

An aside is usually a brief diversion from the main current of a scene, whereas this one alters our whole sense of what we are seeing. Cassio and Desdemona, both of whom we have been enjoying and admiring, are seen as if through a lens that tints their pleasure and courtesy with Iago's hatred. His little litany of bitterness and spite is interrupted, as it is turning excremental, by Othello's trumpet, but in the moment of reunion that follows, the lens, so to speak, is still in place. Iago is both figuratively and literally between us and the happy couple—again the blocking that keeps him downstage seems very clearly indicated by the demands of the text—and their protestations of love are accompanied by his whispered promise of mischief:

> O, you are well tun'd now,
> But I'll set down the pegs that make this music,
> As honest as I am.
>
> [2.1.199–201]

The special relationship created by direct address is beginning to turn uncomfortable. While we might have liked to watch Othello's happiness and enjoy his eloquence as we did in the first act, the addition of Iago's commentary intrudes a perspective that we have no power to ignore or refuse. After the others leave we see Iago toying once more with Roderigo, and then, in a pattern that is becoming familiar, the stage is clear and he is left with us. He has been indulging in specious and denigrating speculations for Rod-

erigo's benefit and goes on in the same vein with us, as if we were
equally gullible and manageable:

> That Cassio loves her, I do well believe't;
> That she loves him, 'tis apt and of great credit:
> The Moor, howbe't that I endure him not,
> Is of a constant, loving, noble nature;
> And I dare think he'll prove to Desdemona
> A most dear husband: now I do love her too,
> Not out of absolute lust, (though peradventure
> I stand accountant for as great a sin)
> But partly led to diet my revenge,
> For that I do suspect the lustful Moor
> Hath leap'd into my seat, the thought whereof
> Doth like a poisonous mineral gnaw my inwards,
> And nothing can, nor shall content my soul,
> Till I am even with him, wife, for wife:
> Or failing so, yet that I put the Moor,
> At least, into a jealousy so strong,
> That judgement cannot cure; which thing to do,
> If this poor trash of Venice, whom I trash
> For his quick hunting, stand the putting on,
> I'll have our Michael Cassio on the hip,
> Abuse him to the Moor, in the rank garb
> (For I fear Cassio with my night-cap too)
> Make the Moor thank me, love me, and reward me,
> For making him egregiously an ass,
> And practicing upon his peace and quiet,
> Even to madness: 'tis here, but yet confus'd;
> Knavery's plain face is never seen, till us'd.

> [2.1.281–307]

Some of this is patently ridiculous, and we might well suspect that
it is laced with the same contempt for us that Iago feels for Roderigo, but the convention of direct address as "honest" is so strong,
and we are so drawn to the idea of seeing and knowing more than

the other characters by being privy to Iago's schemes, that we tend, I think, to swallow it with sober faces. The impudent assertion that Iago thinks Cassio might also have cuckolded him might make us laugh and dismiss Iago's claims in different circumstances; here we tend to let it go by, maybe with a mental note to wonder about it at greater length at some future opportunity. Our sobriety and our assent are partly based on our awe at Iago's ability to confect one lie out of another and partly at our growing sense of his capacity for evil. That we can experience kinship with such a mind, recognizing its echoing of our own worst behavior, is horrifying too.

A herald reads Othello's proclamation, and we move into the first phase of Iago's renewed machinations. After sending Cassio out to bring the gallants in, he has a moment to check in with us and in effect keep us posted on exactly what he's up to:

> If I can fasten but one cup upon him,
> With that which he hath drunk to-night already,
> He'll be as full of quarrel and offence
> As my young mistress' dog ... Now my sick fool
> Roderigo,
> Whom love has turn'd almost the wrong side outward,
> To Desdemona hath to-night carous'd
> Potations pottle-deep, and he's to watch:
> Three lads of Cyprus, noble swelling spirits,
> That hold their honors in a wary distance,
> The very elements of this warlike isle,
> Have I to-night fluster'd with flowing cups,
> And they watch too: now, 'mongst this flock of
> drunkards,
> I am to put our Cassio in some action
> That may offend the isle. —But here they come:
> If consequence do but approve my dream,
> My boat sails freely, both with wind and stream.

[2.3.44–59]

This is reassuring in one sense because it is so businesslike. Instead of attributing questionable motives and attitudes to other characters and himself, Iago simply sets out the details of his plan. His hatred here takes the relatively bearable form of sarcasm, and if our relationship with him makes us uncomfortable, we are at least on a more straightforward footing. Before he begins to act his part, the actor explains it and the action, and that kind of exposition addresses itself not so much to his inner feelings as to simple clarification of the action.

The plan succeeds beautifully, Iago's boat sails freely, and we are not alone with him again until the end of the scene and the act, after he has reassured Cassio and advised him that the best way to regain his lost lieutenancy is by getting Desdemona to plead his case. That advice takes us back to the larger plan, twice stated, of making Othello jealous of Cassio, and we realize where things are headed. We don't need any explanation from Iago, but that doesn't mean he'll neglect the opportunity to deepen our complicity, and he begins by teasing us:

> And what's he then, that says I play the villain,
> When this advice is free I give, and honest,
> Probal to thinking, and indeed the course
> To win the Moor again?
>
> [2.3.326–30]

The actor who plays Iago can pause here and wait for a reply. We're not likely to respond, though we can scarcely enjoy his point in the way he does.

> For 'tis most easy
> The inclining Desdemona to subdue,
> In any honest suit; she's fram'd as fruitful
> As the free elements: and then for her
> To win the Moor, were't to renounce his baptism,
> All seals and symbols of redeemed sin,

His soul is so infetter'd to her love,
That she may make, unmake, do what she list,
Even as her appetite shall play the god
With his weak function.

[2.3.330–39]

The examples and images he uses here are very much in character.
Renouncing one's baptism and redemption is precisely the kind of
activity this villain can imagine with relish, and the images of the
enfetter'd soul and of the woman playing the god, combining power
and sexual appetite, are images of domination that we can understand would appeal to him. Now he resumes his teasing:

How am I then a villain,
To counsel Cassio to this parallel course,
Directly to his good? Divinity of hell!
When devils will the blackest sins put on,
They do suggest at first with heavenly shows,
As I do now; for while this honest fool
Plies Desdemona to repair his fortunes,
And she for him pleads strongly to the Moor,
I'll pour this pestilence into his ear,
That she repeals him for her body's lust;
And by how much she strives to do him good,
She shall undo her credit with the Moor;
So will I turn her virtue into pitch,
And out of her own goodness make the net
That shall enmesh 'em all.

[2.3.339–53]

The plan is given here in more detail, but the main emphasis is on
the perverse and characteristic relish of mixing good with evil, first
by making sound advice the source of his villainy, then by using
the goodness of other characters, Desdemona especially, as the
source of their destruction. Again, just how unsettling we find this
will vary from spectator to spectator and from production to pro-

duction, but I think it's fair to say that it furthers our close relationship with Iago at the same time that it fills us with fear. Roderigo enters at this point, a slight variation on the established pattern of having his exits precede Iago's soliloquies, and after dispatching him, Iago has a few more thoughts for us:

> Some things are to be done.
> My wife must move for Cassio to her mistress,
> I'll set her on.
> Myself a while to draw the Moor apart,
> And bring him jump when he may Cassio find,
> Soliciting his wife: ay, that's the way,
> Dull not device by coldness and delay.
>
> [2.3.372–78]

Again, the emphasis is practical—a short list of things to do—and he closes with a neat couplet, rounding off the scene and, once more, the act. Sometimes Iago's very wordings are used to intensify our consciousness of how he operates and increase our intimacy with him. The phrase he uses here—"to draw the Moor apart"— is almost the same as the one he employs in the next scene while appearing to be helpful to Cassio: "I'll devise a mean to draw the Moor / Out of the way" (3.1.37–38). Cassio's statement to us after Iago exits—"I never knew a Florentine more kind and honest"— has a comparable effect, of binding us to Iago and separating us from the other characters, even as it increases our revulsion at the way viciousness can disguise itself as goodness.

As act 3, scene 3, gets under way, there is little need for further confidences from Iago. We know his intentions and purposes very fully by now, and we can watch his skillful manipulation of Othello with a full sense of what it means to him to be able to practice on his victim so effectively. His direct address to us, when it does come, continues to have the special quality of binding us in a conspiracy of knowledge as his unwilling accomplices. Othello speaks alone, to himself and in effect to the audience, at 262–83, to muse on what he has heard and to go from "If I do prove her haggard" to "I am abus'd and my relief / Must be to loathe her" to "If she be false, O, then heaven mocks itself, / I'll not believe it." This is more inward and less communicative or manipulative than Iago's address to us, but the main reason that it does not serve to increase our intimacy with Othello comes from the distance that our special knowledge creates. Thanks to Iago, we know too much to feel close to the other characters when they exhibit their ignorance of his nature and his devices. The same effect surrounds Emilia's little speech to us at 294–303, when she has found the handkerchief. Our relationship to Iago has in fact become so important and so binding that soliloquies and asides by other characters lose their potential effect, whereas he can reopen his teasing habit of confiding in us whenever he has a mind to:

> I will in Cassio's lodging lose this napkin,
> And let him find it: trifles light as air
> Are to the jealous, confirmations strong
> As proofs of holy writ; this may do something.
> The Moor already changes with my poison:
> Dangerous conceits are in their natures poisons,
> Which at the first are scarce found to distaste,
> But with a little act upon the blood
> Burn like the mines of sulphur: I did say so:
> Look where he comes, not poppy, nor mandragora,
> Nor all the drowsy syrups of the world,
> Shall ever medicine thee to that sweet sleep
> Which thou owedst yesterday.

[3.3.326–38]

Iago is riding high here, and we are forced to ride with him. While the situation nearly gets away from him a few moments later, he will turn the handkerchief to effect, and his success with Othello will be even more rapid than he appears to have anticipated. The play moves forward now to a series of painful and degrading experiences—Othello's swoon and easy gulling as he watches Iago and Cassio conversing at a distance; the public striking of Desdemona; the scene in which Othello, interrogating Emilia and accusing Desdemona, pretends he is in a whorehouse; the appeal for help to Iago by Desdemona and Emilia; the "willow" scene; the ambush in which Cassio is wounded and Roderigo treacherously killed by Iago; and finally the murder of Desdemona. Through all of this we have just a few brief comments from our strange partner to remind us how much we share his perspective. In act 4, scene 1, he has three lines as he stands over Othello's prostrate body:

> Work on,
> My medicine, work: thus credulous fools are caught,
> And many worthy and chaste dames, even thus
> All guiltless, meet reproach.
>
> [4.1.44–47]

A few lines later, after Othello has withdrawn, Iago has a ten-line speech in which he explains how the upcoming scene will work, a speech we need not examine here because it is fundamentally the same as his speech preparing us for the drinking scene in act 2.

In the last act Iago confides in us twice during the ambush scene. The longer speech is of some interest because it returns, for the last time, to the question of his motivation:

> I have rubb'd this young quat almost to the sense,
> And he grows angry now: whether he kills Cassio,
> Or Cassio him, or each do kill the other,
> Every way makes my game; live Roderigo,
> He calls me to a restitution large,
> For gold and jewels that I bobb'd from him,
> As gifts to Desdemona:
> It must not be; if Cassio do remain,
> He has a daily beauty in his life,
> That makes me ugly: and besides, the Moor
> May unfold me to him; there stand I in peril:
> No, he must die, be't so, I hear him coming.
>
> [5.1.11–22]

The motivation I refer to is the remark about the daily beauty in Cassio's life that makes Iago ugly. Some commentators have felt that of the motives provided by Iago, this is the most revealing, a confession of envy for those who are morally and spiritually superior to him. It is certainly a deeper motive than the others instanced, and one that fits with a number of other details in Iago's character and behavior, but there is reason to be cautious about *any* such explanation from Iago. For one thing, we are very weary and pained by this point, waiting for some kind of relief from our unwilling relationship with Iago and the chain of dreadful events he has engineered; it's not at all clear to me that we are apt to be very interested in new revelations of his motivation. If Shakespeare has saved such a revelation for this juncture, his timing has been questionable at best.

Iago's final "confidence" is a line and a half, an aside as the scene closes:

> This is the night
> That either makes me, or fordoes me quite.

[5.1.128–29]

What I would remark about this is its essentially misleading emphasis, one that has always been present in Iago's dealings with us: that there is some end or goal to his mischief making. Originally that end seemed to be to get Cassio's place while pluming up his own will in double knavery, but when Iago has gained that he shows no sense of having accomplished what he set out to accomplish. One begins to feel that for him it is the activities of manipulation and torment themselves, rather than some completed state of affairs or realized goal, that drives him on. Of course the play is approaching its catastrophe and close, and in that sense Iago can expect either to escape exposure or be caught, but even when the exposure is complete, there is some question, to my mind, as to whether it "makes" Iago or "fordoes him quite." That question is bound up with the fact of his refusal to speak, his famous silence.

If having Iago confide in us so extensively was a brilliant and risky stroke on Shakespeare's part, then having him fall silent and refuse to explain himself in the final scene is the perfect completion of the pattern. The reasons that can be suggested for it are many. In the first place, it is our emphatic release from the terrible closeness of our relation to him. Since we have not been able to choose to forfeit this relationship, it takes an act of will on his part to terminate it, and the less casual that is, the more we will recognize and welcome it. In the second place, the way must be cleared for a close attention to what Othello will do and say. We may never be able to rid ourselves completely of Iago's negativity; it has burned like the mines of sulphur in our blood. But we must, as far as possible, make room for whatever recognition and self-judgment Othello is capable of at this point, and the idea that Iago should comment on it, either privately to us or publicly to the assembled witnesses to Othello's final moments, is nearly unbearable. If nothing else, his self-imposed silence is dramatically convenient, not to say necessary.

But this is only part of the story. Iago's silence, seen in characterological terms, ought to lead us to further recognitions about our peculiar relation to him. If it is a refusal to explain himself to the assembled company, it is also, in a curious way, his farewell and withdrawal from us. Any relief we might have had from the sharing of the knowledge he and we have been painfully privy to throughout the course of the play is definitively withheld. Note his exact words:

> Demand me nothing, what you know, you know,
> From this time forth I never will speak word.

> [5.2.304–05]

There are three immediate reactions to this. Lodovico says, in surprise, "What, not to pray?"; Gratiano says grimly, "Torments will ope your lips," an assertion we may be allowed to doubt; and Othello says, surprisingly, "Well, thou dost best," turning suddenly aside from the need for explanation and toward the business of his own suicide.

And what about us? In one sense we can say "Well, thou dost best," because we are relieved to have this unholy accomplice and confidant at last shut up. But we should also recognize that Iago's silence closes his relation to us in a way that leaves a number of important matters unexplained and unresolved. Our relation to him, finally, is much the same one that the other characters had. And this is amazing when you consider it against the convention of aside, direct address, and soliloquy. It was the amount of confiding in us that Iago indulged in that was supposed to mark off our relation to him as a special one. But that, of course, is what Roderigo thought. And Cassio. And Othello. And presumably Emilia. To them he was "honest" Iago, whom we knew to be false. To us he was *honest* Iago who had so many explanations for his behavior and confided them so freely to us. He has cheated and tricked us, too. He has done exactly what he has told us he would do, but his attempts to account for his reasons have been misleading or specious. And we do not find it easy to admit the extent of our gulling. We may find it more comfortable to continue probing Iago's motives and acting as though he has explained his evil to us adequately if only we can locate the passage that is to be trusted. In his essay on Iago A. C. Bradley warned himself and his readers "not to believe a syllable that Iago utters on any subject, including himself," but he wasn't able to act consistently on his own advice.[9] It is in fact very difficult to treat Iago consistently. He is both real and unreal. Our involvement with him has been a trick in one sense but a genuine revelation on the other, since it has helped us experience evil as total deception in a fashion that is surely unique.

That trick, that device, is in the end perhaps too effective. For the challenge Shakespeare offers us in the final moments of the play is that we recognize, consciously or unconsciously, what has happened, and dissociate ourselves from the practical joke Iago has played on us in order to restore our sympathies and allegiances to the characters with whom they properly belong, Emilia and Cassio and Desdemona and, yes, Othello. To do this with rapidity, to stop being Iago and mend our more wholesome allegiances that decisively, is by no means easy. Othello helps us by regaining his former eloquence, his marvelous storytelling ability and magnetic way with an audience. And Emilia helps us by her courage and her sudden spiritual firmness. But how easy to go on being Iago and remark that Othello is, say, cheering himself up, in T. S. Eliot's phrase. If we all, like Coleridge, have in us a smack of Hamlet, we certainly have a smack of Iago too, and it is not easily dismissed or suppressed. What we know, we know. Even this discussion of mine, dwelling so extensively on the character, succumbs to the fascination of Iago and his trap, his point of view. But at least it avoids some of the traditional pitfalls of *Othello* criticism. It does not try to decide whether Iago's evil is plausible or abstract, and it does not worry the matter of his motivation half to death. It grants him his mystery without ceding the whole of the play to him or letting his poison finally taint our view of all the characters and events.

Once more, then, we have a tragedy that takes its richness from a central and informing tension. On the one hand we see a tragic hero whose eloquence, firmly established in his abilities as a narrator, is lost and regained, with a loss that is deeply painful and a regaining that, if it does not redress the loss, aids in our understanding and acceptance of it. On the other hand we see a villain who insists on using the convention of aside and direct address to make us his unwilling accomplices, a relationship so problematic that it deepens the pain of experiencing the play and confuses us about our ultimate allegiances.

The contrasting poles of this tension are not as sharply stylistic and structural as they were in *Hamlet,* but that is the most convenient way of categorizing them. Othello's eloquence and narrative mastery must be understood as genuine, even though Iago will try to convince us that they are bombast; at the same time, it is Iago's staging opportunities and the special relationship he constructs that are crucial to his success with us; his exploitation of that relation, like first-person narrative, is fundamentally structural. Indeed, the *content* of Iago's speeches, as I have tried to suggest, is often specious and misleading, a mask rather than a face, a device for deception and manipulation rather than a source of meaning and truth. We finally learn so little about Iago's motivation from the supposed confessions he makes to us that it is tempting to regard him as a device instead of a character. If he is a character—and I think he is a great one—he is one who tricks and manipulates us as thoroughly as he does his various gulls in the play, using a device we have learned to trust as a special source of truth and inner meaning. His silence, then, is as appropriate at the close as is his master's last burst of narrative and bloody punctuation mark. And his words, "What you know, you know," may well be addressed to us, with an irony that cuts deep. What do we know? Some people never recover from Iago's trickery. We owe it to Othello, to Emilia, even to Roderigo, to try, so that we can recover our ability to hear Othello's story and stories, one last time in the final scene, and over again each time we see or read the play.

Chapter Three

The Maps of
King Lear

The very first scene of *King Lear* alerts us to an oddly dual world. On the one hand we hear about the potential division of the British kingdom. On the other we discover that this momentous political decision seems to depend on the king's "affecting" one or another party, and we will shortly see the question of the nation's boundaries and rulers settled by an uncomfortably intimate test of love. Meanwhile, by way of exposition for a second plot, Gloucester's "fault" in Edmund's conception is brought to light, or to smell, after nine years of Edmund's "being away," and Gloucester is talking, with a certain amount of blustering pride, about his having to "blush to acknowledge" the kind of conduct that produces illegitimate children. We are seeing old men in power and learning about their whims and faults. This means we must take in public and private issues simultaneously, and the rest of the play will continue to ask us to respond in just such a dual fashion.

Successful tragedy must combine scope with intensity. The scale of action should feel sizable, involving the destinies of communities and nations as well as individuals. We expect a magnitude that will allow us to generalize about questions of human nature, fate, and existence; but the tragic action must also possess intimacy, drawing us into the sufferings and insights it produces. We must learn, close up, what it feels like to be Antigone, Faustus, Hamlet, which means that the play must find ways to articulate their inner lives. Every tragedy reflects this tension between expansiveness and intimacy, and no two tragedies resolve the conflicting impulses in quite the same way. What seems distinctive about *King Lear* is its stretching of the tension, its determination to be somehow more capacious than other tragedies and at the same time to reach a new degree of psychological intensity. The stretching tests the actors, the theatrical medium, and the genre itself. It is both exhilarating and frightening. To trace it is, I think, to encounter the very heart of the play's achievement.

This chapter will reverse the order of previous chapters, taking up structural questions first, in terms of the play's peculiar expansiveness, and then turning to stylistic issues, particularly as they bear on the psychological and spiritual emphases of the play. To say that *Lear* has a public structure and a private style is to oversimplify the matter considerably, but it points the direction this discussion will take.

THE MAP OF ENGLAND

When Hamlet leaves Elsinore, we do not go with him. We await his return, meanwhile observing the developing intrigues at the claustrophobic Danish court. Similarly, once the main characters of *Othello* have voyaged to Cyprus they settle down in close proximity to each other to play out the painful completion of their story. The point is that tragedy usually involves close quarters and a single setting. *Macbeth*, despite a scene laid in England and a marching forest, does much to confirm this tendency. Against it we may measure the enlarging of *Lear* through multiple settings and a good deal of action that is "outdoors."

The sweeping action of *Lear*, signaled from the outset by the talk of dividing the kingdom and by Lear's first major prop, a map of England, takes in the whole of Britain, from as far south as

Cornwall to as far north as Albany (the area north of the Humber, including southern Scotland), from Gloucester in the west to Kent and Dover in the east. Lear's court may be located at Leicester, which he is traditionally said to have founded and to have been buried in, or it may be London. That scarcely matters. What does matter is the way he moves around, along with the rest of the characters, from one locale to the next, until the eventual gathering of the dramatis personae around Dover for the battle with Cordelia's invading French army.

Indeed, Shakespeare had the option of expanding the action to France as well, if he had wished to. Previous versions of the story had the king fleeing to France and reuniting with Cordelia before his return with her army. The playwright shrewdly passed up this opportunity for geopolitical enlargement in favor of a more daring and impressive kind of expansiveness: he sent his tragic hero, who begins early on to fulfill the characteristic pattern of increasing isolation and suffering, out onto the desolate heath and into the now-famous storm. This "outdoor" variation on the tragic hero's plight was among Shakespeare's most brilliant innovations, both in the story as he had received it and in the opportunities presented by the genre of tragedy. The hero, normally trapped or enclosed, is instead exposed: to the elements, to the wilder parts of his kingdom, to the unruliness of his insanity, and to the lower orders of a society he has never really known. Never mind going abroad. The features of Lear's kingdom represented by "poor pelting farms and villages," by hovels, and by beggars like Poor Tom, create an imagery, in the theater and in the text, which harbors precisely the duality of expansiveness and intimacy that Shakespeare seems to have been seeking.

We are already glancing at *King Lear*'s eclectic way with genres. *Lear* borrows from the history plays of its time the habit of moving characters among locales that were the historical sites of battles, treaties, abdications, coronations, and deaths. Audiences associated this structural practice with geopolitical issues and with epic questions of national welfare and the vicissitudes of national history.

For all its historical distance—Holinshed tells us that "Leir the sonne of Baldud" began his reign in 3105, that is, in the Bronze Age and before the birth of Christ—this play cues its audience to political and governmental concerns much more firmly and readily than does *Hamlet,* usually regarded as an intensely political play. It deals with English history in terms of the monarchy and the power struggles surrounding it in a fashion they had come to associate with the chronicle plays.

King Lear also borrows, as I have argued elsewhere, from a less familiar genre, the pastoral.[1] Sending Lear out onto the stormy heath enacts a pattern most familiar from pastoral romance narratives—some of which had been successfully staged—in which one or more characters undertake a sojourn in a rural setting either in the interest of self-discovery or to wait out a period of injustice and misrule in their own society. *As You Like It* is a familiar instance of staged pastoral romance with a comedic emphasis. The similarities in the plot of *Lear* are of course joined with startling differences. Instead of an idealized rural locale, a forest of Arden, we get the inhospitable heath. Instead of the reassuring loss-and-renewal pattern of romance, we get simply loss and more loss. Instead of the affirmative self-discoveries of characters like Rosalind and Orlando, we get the insanity and suffering of Lear and Gloucester, ruined pieces of nature who cannot look to the rural life or the rhythms of seasonal recurrence to protect them from the cataclysms that beset their world. If *Lear* is to be called an antipastoral, we must recognize that the term is valid insofar as a familiar design from pastoral narrative and drama is enacted with meanings sharply opposed to the standard versions.

While *King Lear* risks dispersing its tragical characteristics among historical and pastoral possibilities, it also, as is now well known, partakes heavily of the comical, thus completing the possibilities envisioned by Polonius's famous tetrad. Here again we must look especially to a structural feature, the double plot, extremely familiar by the time of *Lear*'s writing as a feature of stage comedy and never, so far as I know, previously used in tragedy. If the double plot, along with the romance and chronicle elements, leads audience expectations away from the tragic, it also helps to create our sense of the play's unusual size and scope. The Lear and Gloucester plots interweave and mirror each other very satisfyingly, although we must keep a large number of issues and actors straight given that Lear's struggles with his three daughters and their husbands and servants, combined with Gloucester's relations with his two sons, entail a great many events enacted by a good number of different people. Shakespeare manages some nice economies by having Kent return as Caius, by having Edgar "double" as a mad beggar on Lear's heath, and by making Edmund the lover who helps bring out the corruption of both evil daughters, but on the whole he seems content not to greatly streamline or subsume the features of either story. He willingly peoples his stage with a large number of characters, accepting the complications entailed in fully developing two stories.

A lesser playwright faced with the task of juggling four major generic possibilities would certainly have failed miserably. It seems rather like trying to go off in four directions at once. But Shakespeare appears to enjoy the challenge of making all directions ultimately point north, toward tragic insight. A good example of how he manages this effect may be found in the third act, which contains the famous heath scenes and the blinding of Gloucester. We shuttle back and forth between two locales, Lear's heath and Gloucester's castle, but because the locales conjoin—Gloucester comes out to find Lear and aid him, which is the act that leads to his blinding—they do not seem significantly contrasted in meaning or tone. Indeed, the tragic impact of Lear's suffering and insanity, while it is in one sense relieved by our going away from it to follow the intrigues of Edmund against his father, is finally compounded by events which correspond in their horror and intensity to what we have been seeing in the king's story. Similarly, Edgar's somewhat bewildering adoption of the role of Poor Tom helps bind the plots even as it serves to underline meanings about both Lear's and Gloucester's previous failures to understand themselves, their worlds, and their children.

Despite the tragic intensification in these scenes, we never lose sight of the historical, pastoral, and comical lines of possibility. The part of the plot that involves the kingdom's welfare and the course of British history is periodically set before us, as in act 3, scene 1, where Kent and a gentleman talk partly about what Lear is experiencing and partly about Cordelia's impending invasion. The pastoral pattern, meanwhile, is enacting itself both in the action of exile and exposure and in the constant talk about nature and naturalness. Comedy has perhaps the slenderest hold in these scenes, but the Fool bravely keeps up his wry commentary, his verbal games and comic patter, underlining the absurdity and folly of the world he inhabits and making the mistakes of identity—Lear insists that Edgar must be a father rejected by his own daughters, and Edgar as Poor Tom identifies his own father as "the foul fiend Flibbertigibbet"—ring partly with the kind of meaning and force they would have in a stage comedy.[2] There is a bewildering mix of effects, more than it would seem possible to take in on one reading or viewing. Anyone hearing the play described theoretically would say it could not possibly work. And yet it is justly famous as one of the greatest moments in our literature, so charged with meaning and emotion that the main reaction it produces is sometimes simply awe.

If the heath scenes prove the play's expansive tendencies by moving the tragic hero out of his normally confined situation and by keeping four different generic possibilities alive, they also promote the play's capaciousness in another important way, by enlarging its social spectrum. It is important to recognize that Lear's encounter with Tom, Lear's newly found concern for "poor naked wretches," Edgar's babbling about his invented identity as a former servant, the servant's revolt against Cornwall's cruelty ("A peasant stand up thus!" is Regan's angry comment), and a host of other references and associations dealing with the social order and the welfare of its lower members marks *Lear* off from previous tragedies in a very remarkable way.

This is not to say that common people do not have roles of some significance from time to time in earlier tragedies, as witness *Hamlet*'s gravedigger. But there is a shift of concern in this play that challenges the previous decorum of tragedy. Comedy was supposed to deal mainly with the doings of ordinary people. Pastoral might show encounters between upper and lower classes, and could have a mildly subversive emphasis. But tragedy and history were concerned with the fates of rulers and those around them; they touched on ordinary lives only briefly or by implication. By asking what kind of loyalty servants were expected to observe, and by exploring the social perspective of beggars and wretches, *King Lear* moves off in a new direction. Its interest in the idea that the humbling of the mighty can lead to new social insights is quite explicitly expressed, first by Lear in his prayer addressed to the poor—"Take physic, Pomp; / Expose thyself to feel what wretches feel, / That thou mayst shake the superflux to them, / And show the Heavens more just" (3.4.33–36)—and then, to drive the insight home, by Gloucester, who welcomes his new state:

> Let the superfluous and lust-dieted man,
> That slaves your ordinance, that will not see
> Because he doth not feel, feel your power quickly;
> So distribution should undo excess,
> And each man have enough.
>
> [4.1.65–69]

These passages reflect a concern about social justice and the welfare of the lower orders that is simply not to be found in earlier tragedies, by Shakespeare or by anyone else. The Russian film version by Grigori Kozintsev (1970), which showed Lear among refugees on the roads or in hovels where other homeless poor had taken temporary shelter, did not so much impose a Marxist perspective as show us how much this tragedy tries to explore social and political travails in terms of their effect from top to bottom rather than simply in terms of their meaning to those who are at the centers of power.

Recognizing this unique and necessarily expansive tendency leaves us less puzzled by the play's unusual interest in characters like Poor Tom and the various servants. A Bedlam beggar was as low on the social scale as one could go; he makes a perfect counterpart to a king.[3] If the Fool stands for Lear's rising consciousness of his personal folly, Poor Tom reinforces his recognition that he has been a poor ruler. Besides knowing his own family insufficiently, he has been badly out of touch with his impoverished subjects. At first he can only account for the Bedlam beggar in self-referential terms: this must be another mistreated father. But both he and Gloucester are on the road to insights about the human condition and the problem of justice that combine reservations about misuse of authority (for instance, "A dog's obeyed in office") with compassion for poverty and unwarranted suffering.

The play's extensive interest in servants used to puzzle commentators, but if we glance at it in the context of an expanded interest in the social spectrum it is perfectly comprehensible. Kent's disguised return as Caius, Oswald's eminence as a tool of Goneril, Edgar's imagined history as a corrupt and lustful servant of Oswald's type, and Cornwall's "peasant" who refuses to condone his master's mutilation of Gloucester—this rich vein of characters, types, and events bespeaks an interest in the perspective of those who serve the wielders of power and must consider and reconsider the meanings of their bond of loyalty and obedience. Again, no other Shakespearean tragedy takes this kind of interest in the relation of the lower to the higher orders of society. The roles of servants and military subordinates do indeed come in for detailed scrutiny in both *Romeo and Juliet* and *Antony and Cleopatra*. In *Lear,* however, the dynamic is different and the concern goes deeper, questioning the institution of service and its meanings more fully. The more profound examination of social questions takes its place among the other expansions of perspective, setting, and genre that distinguish the structure of the play.

The final feature of *King Lear*'s structural capaciousness that I wish to touch on here is its attention to large questions of fate; human nature; and the relation of human existence and social institutions to the natural world of animals, storms, seasons, and a cosmos of sun, moon, and stars. Here of course we verge on style and its functional inseparability from structure, but if we ignore particular features of the language for a moment we can catch a glimpse of the way in which the play's design and construction afford a setting for this interest, which ultimately makes its intensity felt in the language as well as the action.

We are speaking of degrees, of course. All tragedies ask, in one way or another, about the meaning of suffering, the existence of evil, and the place of human beings in the totality of creation. But *Lear* seems able to pose such questions in particularly memorable ways through its double plot, its outdoor scenes, and its symbolic situations and characters. It is exceptionally powerful at generalizing human experience. When Hamlet says, "What a piece of work is a man," by way of launching his thoughtful expression of ambivalence about his own species, he seems to articulate the feelings of Renaissance humanism, both its confidence and its doubt. But he speaks from within a curiously bounded setting, referring to the very theater he stands in (frame, canopy, ornamented roof) and underlining the personal meaning of his comments: "And yet, to me, what is this quintessence of dust? Man delights not me." The enlarged perspective reduces itself to a focus on this melancholy prince, an actor in a theater who is about to learn of the arrival of some "players" and to say, "He that plays the king shall be welcome." The reflexive and concentrated quality of the moment is thrilling, but it is markedly different from the effect that comes from our watching Lear in the storm saying of Poor Tom, "Is man no more than this?" or asking in the farmhouse, "Is there any cause in nature that makes these hard hearts?" or, for that matter, our hearing Edgar tell his father that men must endure their going hence, even as their coming hither. These questions, rhetorical and otherwise, occur in dramatic contexts that expand, rather than contract, their implications. They are centrifugal in intention and effect, moving outward from the particulars of the dramatic action to a resonant representation of human experience in strongly generalized terms.

This aspect of *Lear* is so familiar that we are always in some danger of taking it for granted. Even when we notice it, we are apt to do so on the verbal level, remarking on the play's stylistic habit of philosophical questioning, its generalizations about nature and human nature. But even if we were to watch a production of *King Lear* in a language we did not understand, the images generated by its performance would go far to clarify this expansive tendency. We would recognize that the family and society were being examined from several angles. We could not miss the theme of old age and the way it forces questions about the course of life and the price of wisdom. The king, fool, and beggar in the storm would have the symbolic force they are famous for; and the scene in which the old blind man is led by his son to an imaginary suicide, followed by the pathos of the meeting between blind earl and mad king, would move us partly for its emblematic force and partly for its human reality. We could be deeply stirred by the reunion of father and daughter even if we could not understand a word they said, and we would understand the terrible meaning of Lear's final entrance with the dead Cordelia in his arms simply from witnessing it as a stage image, an emblematic tableau. The point is how much of the verbal articulation of this play is generated from the way it handles character, setting, and action. Even watching *Lear* in pantomime, we could begin to formulate its questions ourselves, to infer the particularities of its text and their philosophical tendencies. The structural expansiveness I have been examining not only opens to a new generic inclusiveness—a different handling of the tragic hero's relation to his setting, a larger interest in society at every level, and a different kind of concern for justice—but also drives toward an emblematic or symbolic representation of human experience that has led commentators to allegorize and directors to existentialize, as if afraid we would not sense *Lear*'s generalized expansiveness unless it was codified by criticism or made emphatic in production.

I have chosen Lear's map of England as the leading image for the play's expansive tendencies.[4] It confronts us at the outset with the play's potential size, but this map is also, of course, important in terms of its inadequacy. It marks the play's concern with the fate of a king and a kingdom. But in its two-dimensionality, its failure to capture the reality of the world it stands for, and its function as an instrument and symbol of Lear's folly (to divide a kingdom was to schedule, sooner or later, fratricide and civil war), it is also a summons for a necessary countertendency in the play, a centripetal force to offset the centrifugal impetus of large scope, eclectic handling of genre, and direct address of metaphysical questions. To that tendency, which I will locate largely in the style, I will assign the implications of another "map," the one that Edgar imagines for Gloucester's benefit, near Dover.

DOVER CLIFF

The counterpoint of *Lear*'s expansive and capacious structural features is a curious inwardness and intimacy in its language. That is not to say that there isn't a substantial amount of public, outward rhetoric as well. We could have expected that. What is more surprising is that we move again and again, by verbal means, to the plane of private thought and unconscious revelation, and the playwright finds a great many ways—in dialogue, monologue and specialized forms of expression (songs, proverbs, riddles, and so forth)—to make these movements feel natural and spontaneous. To do so, he must often stretch the known limits of consistent and coherent characterization and be willing to risk sacrificing large areas of plausibility, both in character and in dramatic action.

We noted earlier that intimate matters mingle oddly with public issues from the play's opening moments. Gloucester has a son "by order of law," but he also has one from whose very existence one can "smell a fault"—a proleptic glance at Gloucester's blindness and Regan's suggestion that he be turned out to "smell / His way to Dover." Lear's staged test of love is dismaying partly because it takes a matter that is normally discussed intimately, if at all—the quality and relative strength of love between children and their parents—and turns it into the publicized means by which the division of rule in a kingdom is to be justified. From the outset, then, characters and situations show a tendency to expose private thoughts and intimate emotions to public view, confusing them with political and social issues from which they are usually kept distinct.

This tendency is affirmed in the reactions of both Kent and Cordelia, the two most admirable characters, to the love test. Instead of waiting for a private opportunity to express their reservations, they make matters worse by challenging Lear's plans in outbursts and rebellions of their own. A kind of compulsive or obsessive drive invades the behavior of every character in this play. Cordelia cannot hide her feelings from her father; her sisters can, but later they will be unable to control their sexual obsessions with Edmund. Kent's loyalty may be admirable, but his bluntness is surely less praiseworthy. He gets himself banished at the outset, just as later, unable to conceal his disgust with Oswald and, shortly after, with Cornwall and Regan, he gets himself thrown in the stocks. Injudicious though his testiness and blunt speech may be, they propel the action each time they are manifested and ensure that feelings that might normally be concealed in the interests of diplomacy and tact will be vented quickly and fully.

Impulsiveness, of course, begets impulsiveness, and chain reactions build. Lear insists on the love test, and Cordelia's and Kent's objections then provoke his excessive responses of disowning the one and banishing the other. Quarrels escalate suddenly in Lear's family, and over in Gloucester's household things are no better, as a father decides on his son's guilt swiftly and on flimsy evidence. In such a world their own self-control and calculation make it easy for the evil characters to seize power. Goneril effortlessly engineers her father's break with her, and Edmund manipulates both his father and his brother with a ridiculous ease at which even he marvels. That goodness should be combined with such childish qualities may strain our sense of plausibility, but the resulting dramatic events hurtle the action forward at a pace that precisely suits the play-wright's needs. By the middle of the play he has his tragic hero going mad on the heath and the hero's counterpart blinded. A more naturalistic treatment could never have accomplished such swift twin crises.

Any consideration of obsessive and compulsive behavior in the characters of the *Lear* world must of course take account of the Fool. The point is not that his inner life is important to us. In a sense, he has none. But his "licensing" means that he can and must speak of things that others suppress by reason of social and psychological constraints. His inability to be on stage without blurting out things most people would be careful to keep to themselves contributes markedly to the atmosphere of revelation and the appearance of disrupted norms in speech and behavior. It is true that the Fool's speech is gnomic, given to riddles, sayings, songs, and little fables. But there is nothing disguised about its obsessive content; we always know what it is aimed at and can translate its general intent, even though we might puzzle over details. The Fool is so given to telling the truth, which includes saying the unsayable or forbidden, that he makes the compulsive speaking that the other characters indulge in seem more natural to us. With such a tongue around, why not say what comes to mind, whatever the consequences? Everyone has a touch of the license that is the Fool's by definition.

Disguise, normally a means of concealment, becomes another vehicle for revelation of inward thoughts and feelings in the *Lear* world. Kent's outburst against Oswald seems to stem partly from a desire to vent every single reaction to the man he has ever had. It would normally be edited in conversation, if not suppressed altogether. And whether or not the speech is "in character" for Caius, or for Kent, it seems to take its rationale partly from a prevailing atmosphere of candor and confession:

A knave, a rascal, an eater of broken meats; a base, proud, shallow, beggarly, three-suited, hundred-pound, filthy worsted-stocking knave; a lily-livered, action-taking, whoreson, glass-gazing, super-servicable, finical rogue; one-trunk-inheriting slave; one that wouldst be a bawd in way of good service, and art nothing but the composition of a knave, beggar, coward, pandar, and the son and heir of a mongrel bitch; one whom I will beat into clamorous whining if thou deni'st the least syllable of thy addition. [2.2.13–23]

Addition indeed; we feel that this is somehow both a thorough revelation of what has passed in Kent's thoughts and an extremely shrewd account of what Oswald is really like behind his bland and capable exterior. It may not, in its sheer excess, quite correspond with naturalistic characterization, but it serves the needs of this play's unique style and design.

Edgar's disguise, as Poor Tom, is even more astonishing for the flood of normally private material it unleashes: astonishing because Edgar's experience can have had little resemblance to a beggar's, and to have gotten inside the character in the way that he has makes Edgar something like a Stanislavskian actor in his creative vigor and insight. Not only does he know the catchphrases and constant obsessions—hunger and demons—of the beggar's present life; he has also invented a plausible past for him, one that he is willing to detail to an unusual degree, again as if to express experiences and thoughts that would normally never see the light of day:

A servingman, proud in heart and mind; that curl'd my hair, wore gloves in my cap, served the lust of my mistress' heart, and did the act of darkness with her; swore as many oaths as I spake words, and broke them in the sweet face of Heaven; one that slept in the contriving of lust and wak'd to do it. Wine lov'd I deeply, dice dearly, and in women out-paramour'd the Turk. [3.4.85–92]

This is partly moralizing, of course; it points back to Oswald. But it harps on the private thoughts, especially the sexual fantasies and obsessions, of the imaginary character in a way that resonates with a sense of what he was like in his inmost self. We begin to forget that Tom is an invented character; the information that comes spilling out seems all too real. We are with him at his mirror, while he inspects his curls and thinks lustfully about his mistress.

What makes Poor Tom's private history plausible to us is of course the character's madness; that is a fiction too, but it releases his tongue and turns his mind inside out for us, just as it did with Ophelia. Stage madness has many functions and meanings, but in *King Lear* it is especially useful, both in Tom and in the king himself, as a means of bringing inner worlds into open articulation. To the physical exposure on the heath in the storm is added a psychological exposure that is devastating to witness.

In terms of *King Lear*'s characterizations, the onset of insanity simply extends the compulsive and obsessive tendencies of the play's cast of characters to their most extreme form. From the perspective of style, of the expressive possibilities of speech, madness makes possible verbal exchanges and figurative textures that were unprecedented in drama in their daring and difficulty. Consider the following moment:

> *Edgar.* Frateretto calls me, and tells me Nero is an angler in the
> Lake of Darkness. Pray, innocent, and beware the foul fiend.
> *Fool.* Prithee, nuncle, tell me whether a madman be a gentleman
> or a yeoman?
> *Lear.* A King, a King!
> *Fool.* No; he's a yeoman that has a gentleman to his son; for he's
> a mad yeoman that sees his son a gentleman before him.
> *Lear.* To have a thousand with red burning spits
> Come hizzing in upon 'em—
>
> [3.6.6–16]

Shakespeare is able, in this brief interchange, to weave together references to Samuel Harsnett's studies of demonic possession in *A Declaration of Egregious Popish Impostures,* Rabelais's vision of how rulers are brought to humbled damnation, a proverb about patrimony and social climbing that is rather close to the bone for the author himself, and a vivid image of imagined revenge.[5] He can do all this because of the way madness—the Fool's professional version, Edgar's feigned version, and Lear's helplessly authentic version—sanctions utterance and references that violate the rules (including relevance, avoiding non sequiturs, and so forth) of normal discourse. We can follow the movements of the characters' minds if we are attentive, but just barely. The impression we get in performance is of something close to the babble in a madhouse—expressive speech untethered to current circumstance and incapable of rational discourse.

Even when only one "madman" is present, this exhilarating and visionary style is ready to dominate and prevail. We can fish in the lake of darkness when only one Nero is fiddling:

> Ay, every inch a king:
> When I do stare, see how the subject quakes.
> I pardon that man's life. What was thy cause?
> Adultery?
> Thou shalt not die: die for adultery? No:
> The wren goes to 't, and the small gilded fly
> Does lecher in my sight.
> Let copulation thrive; for Gloucester's bastard son
> Was kinder to his father than my daughters
> Got 'tween the lawful sheets. To't, Luxury, pell-mell!
> For I lack soldiers. Behold yon simpering dame . . .
>
> [4.6.110–20]

The prisoner on trial for adultery is both imaginary—one of several hallucinations Lear experiences in this episode of his madness—and real, in the person of the humiliated and bewildered Gloucester, who stands or kneels before the mad king at this moment. Likewise, the simpering dame will be any lady who is outwardly prudish and inwardly lecherous, and at the same time one of Lear's hypocritical and appetite-driven daughters. Referentiality is multiple, then, as is tone: the attitude that finds copulation a natural activity in a world of wrens and flies will swing round to intense sexual disgust as the passage considers the simpering dame more fully. We have to acquiesce in these multiple references and contradictory attitudes, saying helplessly, like Gloucester, "And that's true too," as we listen to a form of discourse that becomes more inclusive as it grows less rational. At the same time, Shakespeare puts a brake on our admiration. Lest we consider Lear's raving undiluted holy wisdom, he adds ludicrous mistakes and ironic "truths" like the one about Gloucester's bastard son being kind. We are dealing here not only with the inwardness of Lear—the spilling contents of his crazed and tormented but steadily enlightening mind—but with the private lives and thoughts of other characters, real and imaginary. It is a heady mixture, and it is made possible through the license afforded by stage lunacy and the self-revelations that madmen are traditionally said to be given to.

The stylistic complement to the play's tendency to pose large questions about human fate and metaphysical order seems to me to be its extraordinary capacity to produce expressive force from simple details. Some of these details are nonverbal—a map, a storm, a beggar, offstage music—but many are embedded in the play's language. They give us the sense that many meanings and emotions are gathering around a particular image or image cluster, that everything has come to rest for a moment on a single point and in a precarious balance. Here, for example, is the first mention of Gloucester's cliff at Dover:

> There is a cliff, whose high and bending head
> Looks fearfully in the confined deep;
> Bring me but to the very brim of it,
> And I'll repair the misery thou dost bear
> With something rich about me; from that place
> I shall no leading need.
>
> [4.1.73–78]

Gloucester's errors and recognitions, his despair and attempt to resolve that despair, and indeed his desire to reenact his "fall" in a literal fashion, here concentrate themselves in the fanciful image of a piece of nature that seems to react emotionally to its own height and precipitousness. Looking fearfully into the "confined deep" of his own sin and Edmund's evil is just what the sightless Gloucester has had to do, and the image with which he tries to reify his impulse to suicide satisfies us with its vividness and dramatic force: like Lear's heath and storm it is an attempt to use landscape as a means of expressing spiritual and psychological events, making material realities equivalent to mental ones. It is a sign of Edgar's ingenuity and imagination that, instead of repudiating his father's map, as Cordelia in a sense did Lear's, he takes it from him and revises it, remaps it so that it will not stand simply for horror and despair, but also for a world that is complex and bewildering and yet, ultimately, orderly and beautiful.

The highly expressive images that inform *King Lear*'s language, as is well known, take additional strength from their orchestrated recurrences. We will hear of Gloucester's cliff again and will see him try to cast himself over it. Similarly, the play's great multitude of animal references bring an enormous cumulative force to bear on Lear's question, "Why should a dog, a horse, a rat, have life, / And thou no breath at all?" (5.3.306–07). Behind this question echo Cordelia's recent "Mine enemy's dog, / Though he had bit me, should have stood that night / Against my fire" (4.7.36–38) and Lear's speech on need: "Allow not nature more than nature needs, / Man's life is cheap as beast's" (2.4.268–69). These instances, along with a host of other animal references, help distill and intensify the meanings of Lear's question. In the same way Lear's request a moment later, "Pray you, undo this button," aligns itself with the many references to clothing and apparel as emblems of social injustice and psychological distress. Clothing has moved from having incidental and superficial meanings to carrying the potential of expressing whole lives and personalities. Now it can be used to express the full meaning of human grief. The delicacy of the reference, combined with the weight of meaning it brings, never fails to astonish. As readers we cannot even be sure whether it is Lear's own buttons or one of Cordelia's that he is referring to (performances,

I think, must choose one or the other), but either reading effectively illustrates how style is able to underpin structure with simple and powerful details.

Shakespeare's use of iterative images has been fully explored by other commentators. It has occasioned mention here for the way in which it helps the play balance inwardness and outwardness, the private and the public, the particular and the general. We might have been able to say in advance that a successful tragedy should engage large questions about human nature and its place in the created world. We surely could not have predicted that a reference to a dog, a horse, and a rat, or a request for help with a button, could supply an intimacy and particularity that would enhance those large questions through deliberate contrast. The final moments of *King Lear*, like the opening ones, mix public and private matters in startling ways; this time, however, we have come to the fullest possible sense of loss in both areas, and we must stretch our sensibilities to the greatest possible receptiveness to attend to public lament and private grief at the same time. We have the solemn question of the kingdom's fate and succession before us; inextricably intertwined with it is a father's grief for his daughter, brought forward with an intensity that is almost overwhelming. There's a sense in which Lear's personal grief is quite irrelevant to the historical question of how England will now be governed. There's also a sense in which the succession matters not a jot in the face of Lear's overwhelming sense of personal loss. That neither question *is* irrelevant to us at this moment is testimony to the mutual tension in which they are held by the playwright's art.

Edgar's "map" of Dover Cliff, his expansion and revision of his father's scene of imagined self-destruction, can stand as my concluding example of the play's centripetal and inward tendencies. Unlike Lear's map at the play's opening, this one exists only as a verbal event, a striking example of the play's poetic style. Its reality lies in Edgar's mind and then, by means of its striking articulation, in Gloucester's mind and of course in our minds when we read it or listen to it. If there were a real cliff before Edgar and his father (real, that is, in terms of stage representation) we might be less struck by the imaginative effort behind Edgar's account. Discovering at some point in the scene that he is inventing it, presumably by a combination of memory and sheer (no pun intended) inspiration, keeps us in touch with the ontological status of the cliff; it is realistic, in its three-dimensionality and its superbly chosen details, but as the product of Edgar's mind it must necessarily engross us with psychological meanings:

> Come on, sir; here's the place: stand still. How
> fearful
> And dizzy 'tis to cast one's eyes so low!

[4.6.11–12][6]

Vertigo is of course an individual sensation and a rather private one; everyone has experienced it in some form. Edgar translates the distanced quality of Gloucester's earlier "Looks fearfully in the confined deep" into something we can feel in the pit of the stomach or in the teetering body, led forward by its fascinated gaze. Having drawn us close by this means, he begins to sketch out a vertical panorama that features comparative sizes, a human social order that includes samphire-gatherers and fishermen, and the infinitude of the sea:

> The crows and choughs that wing the midway air
> Show scarce so gross as beetles; half way down
> Hangs one that gathers sampire, dreadful trade!
> Methinks he seems no bigger than his head.
> The fishermen that walk upon the beach
> Appear like mice, and yond tall anchoring bark
> Diminish'd to her cock, her cock a buoy
> Almost too small for sight. The murmuring surge,
> That on th' unnumber'd idle pebble chafes,
> Cannot be heard so high. I'll look no more,
> Lest my brain turn, and the deficient sight
> Topple down headlong.

[4.6.13–24]

We end this, as we began it, with the physical sensations and mental consequences of the dangerous view. Edgar is making the created world for himself, for his father, and for us, but he is making it a matter of one's consciousness of it. We are no bigger than our heads. The brain and the sight lead the body where they wish to. What one feels, senses, and thinks is what one truly experiences, and language is the means one has for mapping that mental territory.

Whether Edgar is trying to deter his father from the plan of jumping or instead creating the space he will allow him to leap into is difficult to ascertain. Neither his one aside, "Why I do trifle thus with his despair / Is done to cure it," which comes after Gloucester's decision to go ahead, nor his subsequent admission of concern about whether Gloucester can survive the event, serves to resolve the ambiguity of the situation here. What does seem certain is that Edgar, through an act of sympathy and imagination, is trying to find his way to the very center of his father's despair. He is recreating, in mental terms and by means of more vivid language, the place that Gloucester has intended both to represent his burden of pain, disfigurement, and remorse, and to resolve it. In that respect Edgar is duplicating his feat of discovering the mental landscapes of Poor Tom, the demonstration of intimacy with another's consciousness and private thoughts that almost made us forget that he was shamming.

Edgar may baffle us somewhat, but he is consistent. More than Cordelia, Lear, Kent, or Albany, he is able to conceal his own feelings and protect himself from the manipulations of the evil characters. Like the Fool, he uses imaginative forms of language and behavior to attack or at least solace his worsened condition. Many commentators find Edgar both feeble and priggish, and on occasion he is indeed one or the other or both, but he is also an artist of a kind, making local habitations and names out of airy nothing and warming himself with the energies and inventions of the mind cast out into a wilderness of exposure and near-despair. His cliff is our cliff because we have come to watch a play. We need to believe that language, used creatively, can alter our condition or at least dress us in the rags of consolation when the wind blows and the storm howls around us. In a play in which most of the characters are wildly and helplessly expressive with language, showing us their pain, humiliation, malice, and bewilderment, Edgar has more than a modicum of control and purpose. He has what Keats, trying to define Shakespeare's genius, called negative capability, the capacity for entering into a reality beyond one's own consciousness. The light Edgar shines in the darkness of the *Lear* world is perhaps a feeble one, but its illumination is unmistakable, and without his map of Dover we would be more lost in the "cheerless, dark and deadly" wilderness of the play than we finally come to feel we are. His concluding words, stripped of all false optimism or easy moralizing, refer our bodies to the physical task of carrying what is heavy and our tongues to the question of how best to use our little crutch of language:

> The weight of this sad time we must obey;
> Speak what we feel, not what we ought to say.
> The oldest hath born most: we that are young
> Shall never see so much, nor live so long.

[5.3.323–26]

Chapter Four

Primitivism and Sophistication in *Macbeth*

After seeing a performance of *Macbeth* at the Globe Theater in the spring of 1611, Simon Forman wrote in his diary:

> And when Mackbeth had murdred the kinge, the blod on his hands could not be washed of by Any means, nor from his wiues handes, which handled the bloddi daggers in hiding them, By which means they became moch amazed and Affronted.[1]

Forman got it wrong, of course. Macbeth *says* he'll never get the blood off—"Will all great Neptune's ocean wash this blood / Clean from my hand? No, this my hand will rather / The multitudinous seas incarnadine, / Making the green one red" (2.2.59–62)—but that's really the extent of his washing problem, and his wife's is imaginary too, not the "filthy witness" that a little water can clear them of, but an imaginative obsession that surfaces in her sleep. In the action, the Macbeths are able to appear with clean hands at the discovery of the murder; in the obsessive and extraordinarily evocative imagery, they are indeed red-handed, but only on a metaphoric and imaginative level.

We could dismiss Forman's mistake as evidence of his bad memory (note that he thinks Lady Macbeth is "hiding" the daggers when in fact her purpose is to make sure they are found), if it were not for the fact that it reflects an extraordinary confusion of language and action, word and deed, that seems to characterize this play. A far more sophisticated observer than Forman, Alfred Harbage, has noted of the passage in which Lady Macbeth says that she would have dashed out the brains of her nursing baby if keeping her word had necessitated it:

> Lady Macbeth's vow is so particularized and vivid that, so far as our emotions are concerned, the baby she says she would slay she has already slain.[2]

A distinction we are used to observing, and one that we know was important in Shakespeare's theater, seems to dissolve here, so that the metaphoric and literal levels of the play interchange and mingle.

This phenomenon makes *Macbeth* very different from its immediate predecessor among the tragedies. In *Lear* the magic of language lies in the way it rebounds from experience, differentiating itself and, as far as it can, compensating for the burden of human suffering in an indifferent world. In *Macbeth* something like the opposite is true. Language and experience keep closing. Prayers are answered, invocations are successful, determinations expressed in thought and language move all too smoothly into deed and actuality. "Come, seeling Night . . . ," "Stars, hide your fires," "You spirits / That tend on mortal thoughts, unsex me here"—it's the *success* of these expressions of wish in merging with reality that strikes us, especially when contrasted with *Lear,* where again and again wish and need articulate themselves only to find no response or corroboration in the action. In *Macbeth* we have clearly crossed over into a world where the playwright is determined to handle the word–deed antinomy very differently, mounting a tragedy in which a new kind of intimacy between these ancient factions, a magical partnership like that of the weird sisters, gives the play its distinctive tone and flavor.

This chapter, like the previous one, will consider structure before turning to style. It will also contain a third section, in which *Macbeth*'s peculiar confounding of act and speech will be considered. The infusions of magic and magical meaning in both the style and structure of *Macbeth* lead finally to the interpenetration that both Forman and Harbage, in their different ways, were responding to. But first, of course, we need to notice the customary differences and apparent cross-purposes of these two elements: the play's design, action, and outlines are unusually primitive for Shakespearean tragedy, while the poetry is markedly sophisticated. Magic ultimately unites these oppositions, but not before *Macbeth* gives its audiences a series of jolts and shocks that make it a particularly unsettling piece of theater, a play so opaque and mysterious, so intimate and yet so strange, that it has even become a particular object of superstition to actors, who prefer not to refer to it by its title.

MOST SACRILEGIOUS MURDER

The first thing that strikes us about *Macbeth* may well be its relative brevity. Commentators have suggested that we may be dealing with a cut-down text, but attempts to demonstrate that significant portions of Shakespeare's total design are missing have been singularly unconvincing. The play seems meant to move swiftly and inexorably, to accomplish itself with an economy of action and a clarity of outline that are striking when we contrast them with *Hamlet, Othello,* and *King Lear.*

This is not just a matter of length. The central action of *Macbeth* feels deliberately simplified when compared with other tragedies. Motivations are clearer, cause and effect are more firmly linked, and the movement through disorder and confusion into costly restoration of natural harmony is extremely emphatic. It is as though Shakespeare had decided to speculate on the origins of tragedy and had produced a kind of prototype, a play that recalls the primitive beginnings of a genre that had become almost too sophisticated for its own good. If we take that conjecture a little further, we may find that Shakespeare's investigation of tragedy's origins discovered two long and deep roots: the ritual of replacing one king with another, an old order with a new one, often through regicide; and the irrevocable nature of time, as expressed in the irreversible human action of murder.

It may be objected that the insight that tragedy has its likely origins in rituals of human sacrifice and the transfer of power from a dying king to his replacement is a modern one, derived from the comparative studies afforded us by the discipline of anthropology. The answer must be that such information is not privileged. Shakespeare had thought long and hard about the institution of kingship, through the writing of many history plays and tragedies. He was also aware of the medieval conception of tragedy as a study in rise and fall, the gain and loss of worldly wealth and power. It would scarcely be surprising to the author of *Richard II, Hamlet,* and *King Lear* to be told that the question of succession and the killing of a king had been discovered as the common subject of a great many tragedies.[3]

What is striking about *Macbeth* is the firmness with which this common subject is framed and presented. Duncan's murder and Macbeth's usurpation of the Scottish throne are surrounded by an array of symbolic meanings and actions—in nature, in the body politic, and in the psychological consequences of the act—that makes its tragic implications unmistakable. Earlier Shakespearean tragedies often break with ritual action and ritual meanings, as when Hamlet turns away from his charge to revenge a regicide with a regicide, or when Cordelia and Kent disrupt Lear's prearranged ceremony of inheritance. But *Macbeth* embraces such possibilities, again and again. A victorious warrior is rewarded by his monarch. That monarch pays him a formal visit, is feasted, and then is murdered in his sleep. Guilt is reified by such means as the appearance of a ghost at a banquet and the depiction of compulsive and repeated behavior while sleepwalking. Solemn and paradoxical predictions are enacted more or less literally. A tyrant is dispatched and his head is brought onstage. The formal, ceremonious, even stylized events of *Macbeth* help us recognize that tragic action, however its origins may be disguised by naturalistic treatment, is apt to have as its deep structure the power struggle that is implied by monarchy, by the fact of human generations, and by social anxiety about the orderly relinquishing and assumption of political power.

— If that is the social dimension of tragedy's origins, there remains a psychological dimension to be explored. The other long root of tragedy, as *Macbeth* seems to posit it, is murder—murder as a human act that is irrevocable, given linear time, and destructive not only to the victim but to the perpetrator. One might argue that murder is present in the play because the act of regicide is a ready means of illuminating the genesis of tragic structure in struggles for power. It seems clear, however, that Shakespeare has gone beyond the notion of killing a monarch in order to gain control of a state. We need only compare his treatment of the deaths of Richard II and Julius Caesar to get at the comparison. Their murders matter, but not in the way that the murder of Duncan does. Duncan is not only Macbeth's and Lady Macbeth's ruler. He is their kinsman, their benefactor, their guest, and, in a metaphoric sense that Lady Macbeth articulates, their father. Killing him in his sleep particularly emphasizes the taboo-breaking quality of the murder: Duncan is not only extremely trusting, he is movingly and frighteningly vulnerable. Thus it is that the guilt that eventually devastates both of the Macbeths goes deeper than anything that could be visited on Bolingbroke or England for Richard's murder or on Cassius, Brutus, and the other conspirators for the taking of Caesar's life. The sense that the Macbeths have plunged Scotland into chaos is sometimes almost incidental to our full consideration of the damage they have inflicted on their own psyches by murdering someone whose death could not possibly be justified. We feel we are in the presence of murder as an archetype of the mistaken human act, an event that is tragic because it cannot finally be reversed, explained, or rationalized. Shakespeare pursues the fundamental meaning of murder further in *Macbeth* than in any other play he wrote.

We speak sometimes of domestic tragedy, recognizing that tragic action may be separated from the fates of rulers. One can find, not only in plays like *Othello* and *Romeo and Juliet* but also in contemporary studies of murder, like *Arden of Feversham,* or of domestic passion, like *A Woman Killed with Kindness,* plentiful evidence that the dramatists of Shakespeare's time understood this generic possibility too. Whether or not we are as apt to think of *Macbeth* as domestic tragedy depends on whether we can recognize Duncan as a victim who is not only a king but a sleeping kinsman, friend, and houseguest. It is Macbeth himself who urges this recognition upon us:

> He's here in double trust:
> First, as I am his kinsman and his subject,
> Strong both against the deed; then, as his host,
> Who should against his murtherer shut the door,
> Not bear the knife myself.
>
> [1.7.12.–16]

Each of these trusts subdivides, so that we might say there's a triple or quadruple trust at work, in which Duncan's kingship is one factor among many that make the deed abhorrent.

There's a kind of binocular vision at work in the murder of Duncan, then. Insofar as it is regicide, it refers us to the social root of tragic action; insofar as it is the murder of an innocent, vulnerable kinsman and guest, it is domestic tragedy, a way of posing the question of why human beings murder and what it does to them. The one event can have both meanings. And Shakespeare works to give them simple, clear outlines, relatively free of the kind of ambiguity that surrounds the central events of *Hamlet, Othello,* and *King Lear.* Duncan's goodness and the absence of any real grievance or justified claim to the crown on Macbeth's part makes both the regicide and the murder of a kinsman morally reprehensible. We know that Shakespeare deliberately simplified his sources to lighten the white and darken the black in his story. He also makes the institution of monarchy unequivocally essential to the health of a country by showing us the reactions when it is threatened, in nature—storms, horses eating each other, and so forth—and in society. There's a fairly steady chorus of comment in the play, coming from old men and various opponents of Macbeth and culminating in the scene in England involving Malcolm and Macduff, that emphasizes the terrible social effects in the body politic that can result from a regicide and usurpation. Shakespeare had mounted much more sophisticated studies of the pros and cons of idealized and absolute monarchy in a number of earlier plays; he casts those complexities aside here in favor of a simplicity that seems to search out and reinforce what we now call archetypes.

The handling of guilt has a similar quality: it is profound and frightening. Macbeth is experiencing it even before the murder, in the form of his dagger hallucination and his vivid descriptions of the consequences of unjustified violence. If we compare it to the guilt of Claudius, who has also murdered a king and kinsman, the difference is readily apparent. Claudius can hide his guilt, from himself and others, and can continue to act efficiently as a king. There's a psychological complexity to his behavior that is both intriguing and satisfying. The comparable helplessness of the Macbeths, he early on and she at a later stage, is striking in comparison. So is the intense detail in which their experience of performing the murder—moving up to it, enduring it, and then moving away from it—is presented. We share the experience with them with an intimacy that is nearly intolerable. The simplification—there is no question about the extent and meaning of their guilt—seems to help clear the way for the intimacy and intensity.

Another major route through which Shakespeare achieves a primitive dramatic structure and an archetypal emphasis in *Macbeth* is by an unusual foregrounding of the human body—its parts, its fundamental needs and meanings, and some of the superstitions and rituals that relate to it. This is an area that the style explores fully too, so that we will be returning to it, but it is essential to the structural design and thus deserves close attention here. Again, the technique I used to distinguish stylistic and structural elements in

Lear can be invoked here: if we were to see a production of *Macbeth* in a language we couldn't understand, the importance of the human body, its presence as an object of fascination in this play, would still come through.

To understand how the body emphasis works in the play, we need to step back for a moment and ask, what are the most basic things we do with our bodies? We wash them, we feed them, we commit them to sleep and its restorative powers. We clothe them. What we take into them that they don't need, we eliminate. We fear for their health and sense their vulnerability. When the blood that is supposed to stay inside them comes out we are frightened and even nauseated. And of course we use our bodies to engender, bear, and nurse children.

When you take that list back to the play, you discover that Shakespeare uses each and every one of those functions to reinforce the play's intensity as a tragedy on the most fundamental physical level, one that involves us deeply because it involves us by means of our own bodily awareness. There is the sleeplessness and the sleepwalking of the Macbeths, coupled with the fact that Duncan and his grooms are murdered, in sleep or at the edge of it. There is the obsession with washing, after the murder, when the bright and sticky hands of the guilty couple must be cleaned if they are to present themselves successfully as concerned and innocent hosts. This obsession recurs powerfully in Lady Macbeth's sleepwalking scene.[4] There are the many references to clothing, often as grotesque or ill-fitting.[5] There are the two feasts. The first is given for Duncan while his host, inexplicably absent from the table, is contemplating murder; we do not see the diners at table, but are made strongly aware of the event by the stipulated stage action at the beginning of act 1, scene 7: "Enter a Sewer, and divers Servants with dishes and service, and pass over the stage. Then enter Macbeth." The second feast, which we do witness, is interrupted twice, first by one of Banquo's blood-marked killers (he hasn't washed) and then by the blood-boltered ghost of Banquo himself (3.4). In England we find our attention drawn to disease and healing by the

discussion of the way the king's touch heals scrofula. Bodily awareness is also greatly heightened by the onstage murders of Banquo
and of Macduff's son, difficult to witness and accept. Toward the
end of the play it is the very paleness in his servant's face that
enrages Macbeth, who calls him "cream-faced loon," urges him to
"prick thy face and over-red thy fear," and finishes by referring to
his "linen cheeks" and calling him "whey-face."

The servant's pallor shows an absence of blood. Before all other
bodily references in this play, there is the presence of blood. The
second scene opens with the question, "What bloody man is that?"
as we meet a messenger who will detail Macbeth's gruesome deed
in battle. We hear about blood all the time, of course, so that it is
a significant feature of the style, but we see it on stage too—on the
messenger, probably on the victorious warriors, on the hands of
Macbeth and Lady Macbeth, on Banquo's murderer and all over his
gruesome ghost. It becomes verbally mixed up with other bodily
functions—with washing ("Except they meant to bathe in reeking
wounds" [1.2.40]); with butchering, cooking, and eating ("his bran-
dish'd steel, / Which smok'd with bloody execution" [1.2.17–18]);
and with wading through a pond or river ("I am in blood / Stepp'd
in so far that, should I wade no more, / Returning were as tedious
as go o'er"[3.4.135–37]). Blood comes in gouts, it smears the
grooms and sprays the murderers, it sticks to the hands as filthy
witness. What horrifies Lady Macbeth is the memory of the sheer
amount of it that had once been safely contained in Duncan's body:
"Yet who would have thought the old man to have had so much
blood in him?" (5.1.38–39).

Shakespeare had not read Freud or Jung. He would not think to
compare profuse and heavy bleeding to the frightening manifesta-
tion of the id. But he lived in a society where brutality was much
closer to the surface of everyday life, and where superstitions about
physical manifestations of spiritual guilt in phrases like "murder
will out" and "blood will have blood" were meant much more
literally than we would tend to understand them today. Whether
or not he had even been in a battle, he knew that blood from fresh

wounds would steam in cold air, so that a bloody weapon would appear smoking hot. He knew that the blood of a victim, spattering the murderer, expressed their kindredness, their eternal relatedness, making them "blood brothers." If killing the king was an event fundamental to the tragic pattern, it could also be linked to the fact that killing was spilling blood, lots and lots of it, and that shedding the blood of a master or a kinsman or a guest was breaking one of the most fundamental taboos a human community could establish. The effect of such sacrilege is to turn things topsy-turvy, bottom side up. The effect of murder is to turn things inside out, to make both murderer and victim unnatural. Murder in general and sacrilegious murder in particular were crimes not only against a social order but also against a cosmic order. They were thought to call forth a pattern of reflexivity—"Blood will have blood"—that was finally both reassuring in its testimony to the existence of cosmic order and inexorable in its working. In this respect, *Macbeth* is a kind of tragic primer, a source book of basic truths and images.

Finally, let us consider how the use of magic also contributes to the primitive and archetypal quality of *Macbeth*'s design. For one thing, magic allows the playwright to reify evil, fate, and guilt in the action and imagery of the play, to bring them before us physically to a degree unmatched in the other tragedies. The idea of constraining the natural by some supernatural means—of testifying to the reality of dark powers that may underlie human violence and accompany excessive ambition, of advancing conjectures about the future, and of recalling that practitioners of magic can protect and curse by the use of charms and spells—is everywhere evident in the play, especially as related to the activities and sayings of the witches. If *Macbeth* were not employing a deliberately simplified tragic structure, the witches might well be thought a blemish or a cheap theatrical effect. It is when we recognize that Shakespeare is exploring the fundamental nature of tragedy that they take a logical place in the play's array of primitive effects.

The witches are the very first characters we see. Shakespeare is careful to limit our sense of their supernatural power and meanings

by emphasizing, especially on their second appearance, their petti-
ness and small-scale evildoing (killing swine, raising storms, in-
ducing insomnia). Nevertheless, it is clear that they have been able
to mark Macbeth out as a victim and potential murderer and that
they can both predict his fate and tempt him to it. Giving that fate
a kind of physical reality, by their own presence and by means of
their predictions and visions, they enforce the idea that theater and
magic are never very far apart. The one knows it deals in illusion
and role-playing, the other takes its methods and its spellbindings
more seriously, as activities that are able to merge with reality.
Shakespeare had explored this terrain earlier, in *A Midsummer Night's
Dream,* and he would come back to it in *The Tempest.* Here he seems
not merely to be serving King James's interest in witchcraft and
demonology, but also to be implying that ritual magic and theater
may have the same origin, the urge to constrain and control reality
by acting out meanings that lie behind and beyond its ordinary
boundaries.[6]

It is not just the witches, of course, who provide the magical
atmosphere of *Macbeth.* We have the hallucinations of the dagger,
Banquo's ghost, the marching forest, the benevolent magic of the
king's touch in England, the horses devouring each other, and Macduff's specialized identity as a man not born of woman. The play
fairly tingles with uncanny and volatile effects, and the magic
spreads in a way that does not allow us to understand precisely
where it leaves off. Thus it is that we have the mystery of the third
murderer, questions like "How many children had Lady Macbeth?"
and the insistence of actors that *Macbeth* be referred to as "the
Scottish play." Those who would think the play merely a melo-
drama or insist that Macbeth is no more than the "dead butcher"
Malcolm calls him at the end are in part reacting to a sense of being
tricked by the magic; they are pooh-poohing the superstitions. Jacobean audiences no doubt had a harder time furnishing their reactions with such skepticism. When Macbeth says, "Stones have
been known to move and trees to speak; / Augurs and understood
relations have / By magot-pies and choughs and rooks brought

forth / The secret'st man of blood" (3.4.122–25), they did not chuckle at his superstitiousness; they considered such things to be true in the same way he did. They might think that King James was a little *too* obsessed with witches and demons, but they could not fault him altogether. Their world was shot through with magical meanings that they might recognize as primitive without being able to dismiss them as baseless. Ours is not all that different.

I once observed that *The Winter's Tale* seems to have been put together by a literal-minded playwright who thought a tragicomedy must be half a tragedy attached to half a comedy.[7] Since we know that such apparent literal-mindedness was the product of a very considerable sophistication about dramatic form and its origins and meanings, it should come as no surprise to us that Shakespeare should write a tragedy that sometimes feels as if it had been designed by a man who has heard that tragedy deals in murder, usually the murder of a king, and who feels that elements like guilt and fate are better off represented directly by the forms and agencies they take on in folklore and folk magic. That the playwright who had already produced *Hamlet* and *Othello* and *King Lear* should make such a decision is a matter of no small interest. It shows us that the play is deliberately structured on simpler and more primitive lines; it does not fully show us why those lines have been used. To answer that question we must also investigate the play's peculiar and powerful language, its immensely sophisticated style.

STRANGE IMAGES OF DEATH

The style of *Macbeth* does a great deal to articulate and reinforce what I have called its primitivism. We would not experience such intense physicality, for example, or carry away such an overwhelming sense of the meaning of the blood, if those matters were not richly detailed and superbly present in the language. But these verbal detailings and articulations are handled in extremely subtle ways, through a poetry that can feel very different from the simple and atavistic structure. To realize this is to understand that *Macbeth*'s style is unusually sophisticated, even for Shakespearean tragedy of the first decade of the seventeenth century, and therefore not a little at odds with its plot.

A great part of this sophistication emanates from the hero. The reason that Macbeth can never be seen simply as a butcher, a vile renegade, or a foolish warrior who is henpecked by his wife and hoodwinked by some witches is because the complexity and subtlety of his mind are realized, through his language, to a very remarkable degree. He is unusually self-aware from the very beginning, alert to the power of mental realities and sensitive, even though he is walking away from an extremely bloody battle, to the horror of the murder he is drawn to contemplate:

> This supernatural soliciting
> Cannot be ill; cannot be good:—
> If ill, why hath it given me earnest of success
> Commencing in a truth? I am thane of Cawdor:
> If good, why do I yield to that suggestion
> Whose horrid image doth unfix my hair,
> And make my seated heart knock at my ribs,
> Against the use of nature? Present fears
> Are less than horrible imaginings.
> My thought, whose murther yet is but fantastical,
> Shakes so my single state of man,
> That function is smother'd in surmise,
> And nothing is, but what is not.
>
> [1.3.130–42]

The reasoning that opens this aside, our first full glimpse of the tragic hero's mind, is specious enough to warn us of his limitations. What may impress us most, however, is the combination of sensitivity to thoughts—which are as real as events to this man—and self-awareness about that sensitivity. Macbeth is distressed by his reaction, but he is also analytical enough to want to generalize from it. Not only does he notice his hair stirring and his heart knocking; he follows his urge to compare this reaction to the frightful events of the preceding battle, where, as we have already learned from the messenger of the previous scene, nothing could dismay him. The conclusion he is led to, that present fears are less powerful than horrible imaginings, is one we may only partly accept: it seems subjective, special to Macbeth. Still, we cannot fail to be impressed by the detail and sensitivity of this man's consciousness. He is introspective and he is wary of the strange interaction between his mind and his body. We know we will follow his history, inner and outer, with interest.

In fact, the story of Macbeth's unruly consciousness is one of the most absorbing plotlines in the play. His sensitivity to the power of his thoughts and his absorption in his own imagination continue to preoccupy and disable him as he and his wife move toward the murder. They lead to further soliloquies, to attempts to dissuade her from their course, to the hallucination of the dagger, and to the drugged, somnambulist state in which Macbeth finally performs the murder. It continues afterward, through the plotting of Banquo's death and the slaughter at Macduff's castle, as it becomes clearer and clearer that Macbeth now suffers from a compulsion to turn himself inside out, to act out every horrible thought he has had as a means of relieving his mental torture.[8] He follows the process with gloomy attention and precise calibration. At a midway point he notes:

> Strange things I have in head, that will to hand,
> Which must be acted, ere they may be scann'd.

> [3.4.138–39]

This is a desperate solution to the present-fears-versus-horrible-imaginings dilemma. His encounter with Banquo's ghost, he has decided, "is the initiate fear that wants hard use." Wading forward in the gore of his murders will, he hopes, cure him and bring him peace and rest. A few scenes later, learning that Macduff has fled to England, he determines to force his imaginings into reality with even greater dispatch:

The flighty purpose never is o'ertook,
Unless the deed go with it. From this moment,
The very firstlings of my heart shall be
The firstlings of my hand. And even now,
To crown my thoughts with acts, be it thought and done.

[4.1.145–49]

Again, what most impresses us is not the compulsion itself, but the acute awareness of it. Even as he turns himself into a dry husk, an empty parody of a feeling human being, Macbeth continues to monitor his own descent, the success, as it were, of his failure:

I have almost forgot the taste of fears.
The time has been, my senses would have cool'd
To hear a night-shriek; and my fell of hair
Would at a dismal treatise rouse, and stir,
As life were in't. I have supp'd full with horrors:
Direness, familiar to my slaughterous thoughts,
Cannot once start me.

[5.5.9–15]

In one sense he is emptied out, having projected his slaughterous thoughts so literally on the world around him. In another sense he is filled up, having supped full because he insisted on turning the taste of fears into a huge smorgasbord of atrocities where he has gorged to bursting. Direness, having now been both inside and outside him, has come full circle and is an old familiar. One meaning of this latter word is the familiar spirit of a witch or sorcerer, one that has taken the form of an animal (for instance, the "Graymalkin," a cat, and "Paddock," a toad, to whose summons the witches respond in the opening scene). A familiar is thus both a material and an immaterial being. Macbeth's state is truly grotesque by this point in the play, and his acute awareness of it is anything but primitive.

The passages in which Macbeth reviews the unfolding history of his consciousness and the strange interaction of his mind and body are also often intensely compressed and exciting in their handling of figurative language. Metaphor is unstable in this world; it exists on levels that shift and transpose themselves continually. A small-scale example would be a phrase like Lady Macbeth's "Was the hope drunk in which you dressed yourself?", in which a personified abstraction shifts suddenly from an intoxicated being to a garment one might wear. A larger example of such metaphoric complexity can be found as Macbeth concludes his plans for Banquo's murder. It is one of many instances of conjuring in the play. This particular spell is not technically necessary—Macbeth is asking day to give way to night, which will happen whether he calls for it or not—but it translates Macbeth's obsession with his own guilt and Banquo's suspicion of it into a wish that night will entail a state where murder and evil have become natural and easy "agents":

> Come, seeling Night,
> Scarf up the tender eye of pitiful Day,
> And, with thy bloody and invisible hand,
> Cancel, and tear to pieces, that great bond
> Which keeps me pale!—Light thickens; and the crow
> Makes wings to th'rooky wood;
> Good things of Day begin to droop and drowse,
> Whiles Night's black agents to their preys do rouse.
>
> [3.2.46–53]

This is extraordinary in many ways—Lady Macbeth is present and Macbeth notes that "Thou marvell'st at my words"—but it has strong elements of familiarity to an audience that has come this far in a performance of the play. Images that link the eye and the hand, and that take up the matter of their coordination, or lack of it, have been before us several times. Macbeth introduced them in his reaction to the announcement of Malcolm's naming as heir apparent:

> [*Aside*] The Prince of Cumberland!—That is a step
> On which I must fall down, or else o'erleap,
> For in my way it lies. Stars, hide your fires!

Let not light see my black and deep desires;
The eye wink at the hand; yet let that be,
Which the eye fears, when it is done, to see.

[1.4.48–53]

The animism—stars hiding their fires, light itself able to see—is appropriate to a world where language has magical performative functions, and the supernatural request, for a kind of eye-hand discoordination, will be fulfilled.

Lady Macbeth's invocation, one scene later, seems to be a careful match:

Come, thick Night,
And pall thee in the dunnest smoke of Hell,
That my keen knife see not the wound it makes,
Nor Heaven peep through the blanket of the dark
To cry, "Hold, hold!"

[1.5.50–54]

Here the capacities of sight and action are astonishingly transferred to the "seeing-eye" knife, acting furtively in a world that is characterized as alert to the danger of evil. Eye, hand, and knife will find their way into the action: in the apparition of the dagger, which Macbeth can see but not grasp, and in the grooms' knives which Lady Macbeth must handle, returning them to the murder scene because her husband cannot bear to look on what he has done. Because of these anticipatory passages, what should be metaphor instead of action will have the force of action:

Whence is that knocking?—
How is't with me, when every noise appals me?
What hands are here? Ha! they pluck out mine eyes.

[2.2.56–58]

This plucking isn't literal, but since the Macbeths have deliberately tried to dissociate eye from hand and knowledge from responsibility, the restoring of eye-hand coordination, characterized as a painful plucking of the one by the other, is nearly as real to us as a literal action. No wonder Simon Forman had his problems with those hands!

By the time we reach the "seeling Night" passage, then, we have already passed beyond the normal borders of what is and isn't metaphor. The references to eye and hand, as well as the invoking of a similar network involving day and night, open up possibilities of analogies that have their own analogies. Normal comparative relationships are being complicated and reversed. If someone asked you whether a hand could be both bloody and invisible, you would say "of course not," but that kind of contradiction has begun to seem perfectly acceptable in the *Macbeth* world. Here, in the fusion the opening set of images provides, day is a falcon, about to have its eyes sewn shut ("seeling") as part of the taming process by Night, a falconer, a blindfolder ("scarf" as a verb is rare, but one encounters it in *Hamlet*: "my sea-gown scarf'd about me in the dark"). Night's scarfing hand is bloody (metaphoric or literal?) and invisible (same question). It is also instructed to cancel, as if legally invalidating, the bond of secrecy and privacy that Macbeth and Banquo share, and to tear it to pieces. By saying that the bond keeps him pale, Macbeth connects the imagery of light and day specifically to the body and its blood, linking the passage to another crucial network of images. In another kind of wordplay, words like "tender" and "pitiful" are used in double senses; here the first is a combining of the physical and the emotional, the second plays with the reciprocal meanings of "to be pitied" and "full of pity." The language is so alive to possibilities and nuances, so three-dimensional, that it does not simply mirror and complement the action but shapes it and gives it a reality it would otherwise lack.

In its second section the passage begins to recapitulate itself. Its next phrase—"light thickens"—joins a series of images of liquid and liquidity to the many images of light. Because Lady Macbeth has said, "Make thick my blood" (another conjuration) and talked of her milk turning to gall, of the milk of human kindness in her husband, and of giving suck to "the babe that milks me," we may get an impression here of light as milk and darkness as a kind of sludgy blood. Later, when we hear the witches making their gruel "thick and slab" (an awful glance, meanwhile, at the network of eating and feasting imagery), or hear Malcolm pretend that he will "pour the sweet milk of concord into Hell," we will associate these images not only with the previous liquid states, with nursing and bleeding, but with light and dark, day and night, as well.

Even in a phrase as apparently simple as "light thickens," then, metaphors are exchanging qualities, forming networks, and rooting themselves more and more deeply in the action of the play. The process would seem like excessive verbal playing, a kind of baroque complexity-for-complexity's-sake, if it were not so crucial to what happens on what can be called the play's literal level, a level of simple experiential continuities—light and dark, day and night, eye and hands, blood and milk. These continuities are transformed into dense, startling metaphors so that they loom out of proportion to their ordinary and elementary nature. The "crow / Makes wing to th' rooky wood": is that another metaphor for the onset of evil, or is it a literal event in the action of the play? I should say both. The adjective "rooky"—the wood already has both crowlike (a rook is like a crow) and non-crowlike (a rook is not the same as a crow) attributes as the crow heads toward it—is typical of the compounding tendency ("droop and drowse," "bloody and invisible," and "cancel and tear to pieces") by which the style intensifies itself and the language begins to rival the action as a reality. In the final couplet of the passage we accept with some tranquility the idea that "good things of Day" are replaced, as part of a natural process, by "Night's black agents," but if we recall that those agents include Macbeth's hired assassins, metaphor bringing us round to action once again, then we can recognize that we are witnesses to a naturalizing of murder in the imagery of the play that is concomitant to the naturalizing of it in the action. In a sense, the action of *Macbeth,* its literal level, is a struggle between two metaphoric paradigms, one that asserts the mastery of "Night's black agents" on an equal basis with "Good things of Day," another that upholds the superiority of love, light, kinship, tenderness, and order. The passage I have been exploring is composed of seven and a half lines. The length of discussion required even to begin to sort out its metaphoric levels and to search out some of its connections to complex networks of metaphoric association and meaning is itself eloquent testimony not only to the figurative inventiveness of later Shakespearean verse, but also to its indissoluble relation to the dramatic action, its tendency to *become* the dramatic action in the case of *Macbeth*.

The vividness and freedom with which metaphor is handled in the play is partly made possible by a willingness to create large and difficult units of syntax, sentences that complicate the reality they report on by multiplying its possibilities and relationships while nevertheless struggling toward a unified vision of experience. I'd like to offer two examples of this taxing and inclusive syntax. Both are ten-line sentences. The first is seldom noticed; Macbeth addresses it to Banquo's murderers in the process of commissioning them:

Ay, in the catalogue ye go for men;
As hounds, and greyhounds, mongrels, spaniels, curs,
Shoughs, water-rugs, and demi-wolves, are clept
All by the name of dogs: the valu'd file
Distinguishes the swift, the slow, the subtle,
The housekeeper, the hunter, every one
According to the gift which bounteous Nature
Hath in him clos'd; whereby he does receive
Particular addition, from the bill
That writes them all alike; and so of men.

[3.1.91–100]

Eighty-five percent of this sentence, we can say, is given over to the trope. Its size allows Macbeth to exercise his smooth eloquence and rhetorical finesse, but it also gives us time to digest ironies the murderers seem to miss—that they are no better than animals in the deed they are asked to do; that a differentiation of the larger class "men" would give them appellations, such as "assassin," that they would be ashamed of; that they will violate, not affirm, bounteous nature by the action they will be asked to perform; and that in their office as ambushing murderers they have neither the dignity or naturalness of a watchdog ("housekeeper") or a good hound ("hunter"). The luxuriance of the figure comes from a luxuriation in the syntax, revealing both the positive aspects of Macbeth (he handles language superbly and keeps its relationships firmly in control) and his negative qualities (manipulation, deceit, and the appropriation of natural order to evil ends). Yet the sentence does not stand out. There are many like it in the play, and their cumulative effect is to habituate us to an eloquence that is partly composed of ingenious and engorged syntactical units.

My second example is much more famous. It comes from Macbeth's meditation on the meaning of the murder. Spoken before the deed, it belongs to a section of the play in which we can still give our sympathies rather fully to the hero. We are struck by its energy, imagination, complexity and moral awareness:

> Besides, this Duncan
> Hath borne his faculties so meek, hath been
> So clear in his great office, that his virtues
> Will plead like angels, trumpet tongu'd, against
> The deep damnation of his taking-off;
> And Pity, like a naked new-born babe,
> Striding the blast, or heaven's Cherubin hors'd
> Upon the sightless couriers of the air,
> Shall blow the horrid deed in every eye,
> That tears shall drown the wind.
>
> [1.7.16–25]

The wild series of personifications, along with the growing hyperbole of this passage, have led commentators to characterize it as almost surrealistic in effect, and to marvel at the ways it connects to other image networks in the play.[9] It is certainly wonderful to consider how the "sightless" (the word can mean "invisible" or "blind") winds are going to blow the deed, like a cinder or dust mote, into every eye, so that the resulting tears reciprocate by drowning the wind. How do you drown the wind? Presumably by a drenching downpour of rain, the kind of foul weather that the witches love, here converted to the service of grief and moral indignation. This is one small ramification of the implications of syntax and imagery in a passage that offers us poetry and eloquence made partly possible by willingness to experiment. This "bright, loud scenario," as a student of mine once called it, binds us closely to Macbeth.[10] Surely moral awareness of this degree, so full a sense of the terrible consequences of unjustified regicide, will turn the speaker away from the deed. To know this much and still carry out the murder would be intolerable. But the intolerable looms ahead, with growing inevitability.

Something like the opposite of this sophisticated syntax can be seen in *Macbeth*'s transformation of ordinary words, by such simple means as iteration and shifting emphasis, into resonant and expressive symbols. We have already glanced at some instances that involve the recurrence of *eye* and *hand* (and concomitants like *see* and *give* and *take*), of *blood* and *day* and *night*. These everyday words become charged with special meanings as they recur in the *Macbeth* world. It is partly a matter of emphasis, partly of context, but the overall effect is peculiar to this play and a hallmark of its style.

Iteration is the simplest way to give words a special emphasis, and some instances of it in *Macbeth* show how daringly the playwright is willing to huddle recurrences together, so that key words almost seem to hang in the air like objects:

> Methought, I heard a voice cry, "Sleep no more!
> Macbeth doth murther sleep"—the innocent Sleep;
> Sleep, that knits up the ravell'd sleave of care
>
> . . . .
>
> Still it cried, "Sleep no more!" to all the house:
> "Glamis hath murder'd Sleep, and therefore Cawdor
> Shall sleep no more, Macbeth shall sleep no more!"
>
> [2.2.34–36, 40–42]

We also happen, in this passage, to be in the midst of some characteristically engorged syntax, but the effect of the iteration of the word *sleep* is like a series of direct and simple blows driving the point home. The word *sleep* occurs twenty-three times in the play, along with *sleepers, sleeps,* and two instances each of *sleepy* and *sleeping*.[11] The lines just quoted can be seen as a kind of node, or nucleus, in which the importance of the word and its referent are ferociously established, with the previous and following repetitions radiating away from it to fill the furthest reaches of the action.

Sometimes these intensive iterations establish several meanings of a single word, as in the famous opening to Macbeth's great soliloquy before the murder:

If it were done, when 'tis done, then 'twere well
It were done quickly.

[1.7.1–2]

Each meaning of *done*—something like "concluded," "performed," and "finished"—is slightly different, though they shade into one another. The effect is partly one of economy, a single word sufficing where two or three might have been used, and partly of three-dimensionality, as if a demonstration of the various facets a word may possess were underway. Again, once the word has been established as a focus of interest in and of itself, its further repetitions, as in "I have done the deed" (*deed* is another such word) and "I am afraid to think what I have done" (*think* and *afraid,* with its many variations in *fear* and related words, are other examples of iteration), resonate powerfully. The two sentences just cited are extremely simple as to diction. There is nothing exotic or unusual about them. They develop their power in the context of iteration and shifting emphasis that the *Macbeth* style explores and achieves.

A list of these ordinary words would include nouns like *air, love, man,* and *time*; adjectives like *dead, full, great,* and *strange*; verbs like *come, know, make,* and *speak*; and adverbs like *here, now, all,* and *yet.* They constitute a kind of counterpoint to the richer and more exotic vocabulary (examples include "the multitudinous seas incarnadine" and "trammel up the consequence and catch, / With his surcease, success") and to the complex, sophisticated syntax. They resonate, as I indicated earlier, with the archetypal emphases of the structure, and by transforming ordinary diction they help to transform ordinary reality and highlight those aspects of it—air, food, sleep, peace, night—that we commonly take for granted until events like murder, events of tragic irrevocability, recast their meanings and make them extraordinary, make them precious or perverted. We have noted the economy of *Hamlet*'s structure, its willingness to repeat and reuse events and situations with unusual thriftiness. In the case of *Macbeth* it is the economy of style that we need to remark, recognizing how the recycling of key words (fittingly, *again* is one of them) can give the play's language its special character and flavor.

When you add up the stylistic characteristics of this play, you find an exaggerating or heightening of tendencies that are always present in Shakespeare, norms and elements that become special in this dramatic context because they have been taken a little further. The rich detailing of the hero's consciousness is not unique to this play. Neither are the preference for engorged syntax, the complex image networks, and the iterative and variously shaded diction referring to fundamental facts of life and nature. It is the aggregation of these practices, along with their emphatic treatment, that constitutes the uniqueness of style in *Macbeth*. That style I have characterized as sophisticated. It reflects the latest currents of poetic fashion of its time—*Macbeth* is very Jacobean as to its poetry—and it calls for the fullest use of the very considerable resources of verbal art that Shakespeare had at his command. How, we might ask, could such a simplified play have such a complex style? Given Shakespeare's practice as a writer of tragedy, the answer must be, how could it not? It is time now, however, to consider how style and action close and even fuse in this play, one more aspect of its uniqueness.

CONFUSION'S MASTERPIECE

Keeping structure and style separate in the foregoing sections has been difficult, sometimes impossible. The truth is that in *Macbeth,* more than in any other play of Shakespeare's, these two elements alternately fuse and play each other's parts. Thus our antinomies—primitive and sophisticated, deed and word, strut and fret (to borrow Macbeth's own bitter division of the two features of stage acting as a metaphor for life)—are held separate only by a kind of pressure that is countered by the play's extraordinary habit of confusing them. In this section I propose to acknowledge this habit, this counterpressure, and to explore some of its unusual and intriguing results.

We may begin by examining some of the ways in which language translates itself into action, so that a word *is* a deed, a fret is a strut. I mentioned earlier that *Macbeth* exhibits a strong interest in the magical performative functions of language. In *Henry IV, Part One,* when Glendower has boasted that he can call spirits from the vasty deep, Hotspur's skeptical reply—"Why so can I, or so can any man; / But will they come when you do call for them?" (3.1.52–53)—mocks the notion that special language can constrain the world or any spirits beyond it. That attitude can be seen as one extreme against which to measure the way vows, conjurations, charms, spells, and prophecies not only matter but also generally succeed in the world of *Macbeth.*

The play's magical speech-acts range from the rather mechanical use of prophecies, riddles, and spells by the witches to highly poetic instances. On the one end of the spectrum are the charms the witches offer as guarantees of protection and immortality to Macbeth. We may wonder why such tarnished verbal amulets would take in so thoughtful and sensitive a man. But he has already been led by the nose by the "promise" of the prophecy that makes him king and that he and his wife take as license and pretext to murder Duncan. The credulity about the prophecy reveals Macbeth's disposition to evil, while the hoodwinking involved in the guarantees about Birnam Wood and a man "not born of woman" suggests how far gone he is by the latter part of the play.

More interesting are the vows and conjurations the Macbeths employ as they move toward and then away from the murder. Lady Macbeth's are among the most chilling:

> Come, you Spirits
> That tend on mortal thoughts, unsex me here
> And fill me, from the crown to the toe, top-full
> Of direst cruelty! make thick my blood,
> Stop up th' access and passage to remorse
> That no compunctious visitings of Nature
> Shake my fell purpose, nor keep peace between
> Th' effect and it! Come to my woman's breasts,
> And take my milk for gall, you murth'ring ministers,
> Wherever in your sightless substances
> You wait on Nature's mischief! Come, thick Night,
> And pall thee in the dunnest smoke of Hell,
> That my keen knife see not the wound it makes,
> Nor Heaven peep through the blanket of the dark,
> To cry "Hold, hold!"
>
> [1.5.40-54]

This is somewhat like Lear's elaborate curse on Goneril ("Hear, Nature, hear; dear goddess, hear!" [1.4.272ff.]), and we can observe that both prayers are in their way fulfilled, but what strikes us chiefly about Lear's is the way in which his request is ignored, deferred, or frustrated, while what strikes us about Lady Macbeth's is the rapidity with which she gets her wish. Her assumption that she can call on evil spirits for such a transformation is not ludicrous because it occurs in the context of her husband's similarly answered conjurings and prayers, such as "Stars, hide your fires" (1.4.50f.) and "Come, seeling Night" (3.2.46f.) as well as the context of the witches' overt and more literally defined magic. We are never quite sure, of course, whether evil spirits literally possess Lady Macbeth as a result of this prayer or whether they are a metaphor for her will and intent. The fact that evil is so palpable in the play does not mean that the question of its origin and operation is unambiguously answered.

Because of this atmosphere of magic and these remarkably successful performative speech-acts, even speeches and descriptions that might not have such a force in different settings take on the same kind of meaning. Two instances must suffice here. The first is Lady Macbeth's famous account of what she would have been willing to do to hold to a vow such as Macbeth has made:

> I have given suck, and know
> How tender 'tis to love the babe that milks me:
> I would, while it was smiling in my face,
> Have pluck'd my nipple from his boneless gums,
> And dash'd the brains out, had I so sworn
> As you have done to this.
>
> [1.7.54–59]

This bears on magical speech in several interesting ways. It acts to reinforce the purpose behind an oath, and is successful in that goal, marking the turning point at which Macbeth agrees to put all his reservations aside and carry out the murder. It also outlines an action that, for all its horror, is offered as less offensive than breaking one's word, so that the nonperformance or violation of a promise or vow is given greater importance than silently braining a baby. By Lady Macbeth's curiously twisted logic, which adds to our sense of the magic, to fail to kill the man, having sworn it, is somehow to kill the baby, or worse. To perform the infanticide she imagines, Macbeth would have to be a woman, an unlikely woman willing to destroy her baby in the very act of nursing it, while its mouth is still full of her own milk. She comes up with precisely the kind of imaginative horror suited to drive him to action, and in doing so she goes beyond the bounds of what we would consider acceptable speech. It is worse than cursing or blaspheming. And it is, as I noted earlier, citing Alfred Harbage, something we may experience as the most violent *event* in a very violent play. If we take it that way we are acknowledging that saying has become as important as doing. Evil consists here in being willing to brain a baby, a willingness that consists of the ability to articulate the thought, both hypothetically—if I had sworn as profoundly as you did, I would have been willing to perform this act—and with unforgettable vividness. Words like "persuasion" and even "manipulation," with its implication of handling and doing by means of saying, scarcely seem to do justice to the power language exhibits at such a moment.

My second example is not strictly a conjuration, vow, or prophecy, but is largely the sort of atmospheric descriptive speech that is quite familiar in Shakespeare's theater:

> Now o'er the one half-world
> Nature seems dead, and wicked dreams abuse
> The curtain'd sleep: Witchcraft celebrates
> Pale Hecate's off'rings; and wither'd Murther,
> Alarum'd by his sentinel, the wolf,
> Whose howl's his watch, thus with his stealthy pace,
> With Tarquin's ravishing strides, towards his design
> Moves like a ghost.—Thou sure and firm-set earth,
> Hear not my steps, which way they walk, for fear
> The very stones prate of my where-about,
> And take the present horror from the time,
> Which now suits with it.—Whiles I threat, he lives:
> Words to the heat of deeds too cold breath gives.
>
> [2.1.49–61]

The address to the earth is prayer or adjuration, but it is followed by the acknowledgment that talking can prevent doing rather than help accomplish it, and the speech as a whole is recognized by an audience as the kind of scene-setting and choric commentary that may be integral to good theater but is not ordinarily charged with magical possibilities or with word-deed fusion. In the peculiar world of *Macbeth*, however, it can be seen as inhabiting one end of a performative spectrum that has the witches' spells and charms as its other extreme. A bell rings just at this point in the play, the prearranged signal the Macbeths have agreed on, and he moves resolutely off to carry out the regicide, embodying his own earlier personification, withered Murder, "alarum'd by his sentinel"; his "words" turn out not to have cooled his purpose but to have shaped and energized it, given it reality in language.

Macbeth's peculiar compulsion to exteriorize the horrors that grow inside him, making his worst thoughts into actualities, must also be considered in this context of words functioning as deeds. A thought need not be articulated in language, of course, but we normally make a distinction (especially in the theater) between what may be said, uttered because conceived in the mind, and what is done. A threat of murder is not the same as a murder, though both may be said to have the same impulse behind them. What seems to happen to Macbeth is that the vividness of his imagination makes him feel victimized by his thoughts in a way that utterance cannot resolve or address. To think of murder and to talk of murder are hallucinatory horrors only laid to rest in the mind by converting them to deeds, though the relief his actions provide is obviously not what Macbeth hoped it would be. Still, the compulsion to act out what may be merely thought or said joins itself to the world of magical language and of word–deed confusion. We now have the possibility of magical *thinking,* with the tragic hero as its vibrant, expressive center.

This issue helps explain, I believe, the strange little scene in England involving Malcolm and Macduff. Before Macduff receives the terrible news of the slaughter of his family—one more demonstration of the great weight words can bear—Malcolm tests him with an account of his evil disposition that, when it leads to a lament by Macduff for the further woes ahead for Scotland, Malcolm retracts, accepting Macduff as a trusted ally. In addition to being an elaborate verbal charade, a loyalty test, Malcolm's hyperbolic account of his potential for evil seems to recapitulate in miniature the action of the play. The key difference between Macbeth and Malcolm seems to be that the one cannot encounter the disposition to evil within himself without an accompanying compulsion to act it out, while the other can put it into words, which are retractable and, in this case, harmless. Malcolm will presumably be less corruptible in power because he can contemplate his own potential for sin, articulate it to himself and others, and then draw back from it. The word–deed distinction, crucial to reasonable human behavior, will be restored under his regime. Language will be less magical, behavior less compulsive.:

> —this, and what needful else
> That calls upon us, by the grace of Grace,
> We will perform in measure, time and place.

> [5.9.37–39]

Recognizing the many ways in which language becomes action in *Macbeth*—and my brief survey has by no means been exhaustive—asks for a comparable glance at action's ability to function as speech and metaphor. The play begins with the witches. Their actions and movements, we recognize, constitute a kind of special language that affiliates itself with their gnomic speech. We hear next about the extraordinary deeds of Macbeth. His actions as a warrior speak louder than words and confer a special identity upon him. A new name will be given to him—he will become Cawdor as well as Glamis—and the earning of that title and the king's conferring of it, which is both an action and a speech, suggests that Macbeth's actions have transformed him and enhanced his identity. Unfortunately, Cawdor is a traitor's name, and, as though it carried its own poison in its very formulation, Macbeth is tempted, when the new name of King appears on his horizon, to deeds which will turn out to be disgraceful and ruinous. Another name, the Prince of Cumberland, will be a "step" he needs to overleap or else fall down on, but by the end of the play his vaulting ambition seems to have taken him past all his given and potential names, to a place where he retains only such generic identities as "tyrant," "hellhound," "villain," and "butcher."

If names have a special value in this world, so do phrases that constitute and even seem to contain crucial attributes. The deed that finally undoes Macbeth, Macduff's news that he was born by Caesarean section, is a report that breaks a spell, another set of words that have given Macbeth the "charmed life" he bears through the equivocation of the witches. His physical death, once his protective spells have been stripped from him, is almost an afterthought. And his beheading seems intended to enforce the word–deed and mind–body splits of the normative world, guaranteeing that tongue and ear and capacity for thought can be divided from the rest of the physical body, just as the spells can turn out to "palter in a double sense," flattering ear and mind without truly protecting the body from its own mortality.

While *Macbeth* shows us a world where language shimmers and looms with a special potency, it also gives us an action in which muteness is sometimes the most eloquent form of communication. Macduff can finally react to the terrible news about his family only with silence, a silence he is urged to break, so as to articulate his grief lest it destroy him from inside. Dumb animals—an owl that attacks a falcon, horses that eat each other—testify by their uncharacteristic behavior to the state of a world disfigured by regicide. The sleepwalking scene, with its pantomimed handwashing, scarcely requires the verbal articulation of Lady Macbeth's guilt to accomplish its meaningful communication. And Macbeth himself acknowledges that he lives in a world where mute objects like stones and trees can bear witness to human guilt. The marching forest which eventually descends upon his castle should come as no surprise to him or to any of his contemporaries. And the silence of Banquo's ghost constitutes a terrifying eloquence that would be spoiled if the apparition began to speak.

Even trying to distinguish words that are deeds from deeds that act as words is difficult with *Macbeth,* so tightly knit are action and style in this play. "A deed without a name," as one of the witches calls their activity around the cauldron, is an action so closely tied to the meaning and function of language that the distinction between sign and referent is no longer useful or necessary. This is what magic means, and this is what *Macbeth* accomplishes in the theater. No doubt Shakespeare sacrificed some possibilities of tension and nuance by pursuing such intensive unity where he had not insisted on it before, but the artistic whole that he achieved as a result is hard to quarrel with. We come back again to the theatrical power of *Macbeth* and the way it embodies the recognition that action and speech are necessary partners in great drama. When Macbeth reflects upon the very medium he inhabits by comparing life to "a poor player / That struts and frets his hour upon the stage, / And then is heard no more" (5.5.24–26), he stands at the center of a complex web of meanings and relationships that depend upon the figurative power of both action and speech for their ultimate success. An actor who is impersonating a rightful king, stands before us recognizing his failure (and the failure of the character is necessarily the success of the actor) and generalizing from it. To arrive at this figurative meaning he has performed a series of actions that have led him to this moment. But to understand fully the implications of his actions he must articulate their meaning in language, language that can finally be used reflexively to frame the frame, the medium of theater itself, and to fully illuminate this moment of candle and shadow, strutting and fretting, sound and fury and signification, not of "nothing," as Macbeth thinks, but of this equivocal "something" to which we are both witnesses and participants.

Conclusion

Let us go back for a moment to some of the contemporary attitudes that have been cited in the course of our discussion of Shakespeare's tragedies. Two of them were eyewitness accounts. First, Henry Jackson, the Oxford student who saw Shakespeare's company perform *Othello* on tour in 1610 (see chapter 2, note 5). Jackson does not say whether he himself was moved to tears, but he admires Shakespeare's company because "non solium dicenodo, sed etiam faciendo, quaedam lachrymas movebant"—not only the speeches but also the actions moved some to tears. There, once more, are the twin elements on which this study has been founded. Henry Jackson may have mentioned speaking ahead of movement because he was a student being trained in rhetoric; he much admired the way Desdemona argued her case before being strangled. In any case, he recognized speech and action as separate components of theater, and he seems to have understood that their balanced effectiveness, as exhibited in style and structure, was a significant factor in the excellence of *Othello*.

Our other eyewitness was Simon Forman who, it will be recalled, confused some things *said* with some things *done* in the performance of *Macbeth* he saw at the Globe in 1611. Less conscious than we of what his reaction might mean, Forman nevertheless faces us toward the same insight: in the acting of Shakespeare's company and in the plays he wrote for them, effective speech and purposive action were so happily interactive, especially in *Macbeth,* that they couldn't always be told apart. We may envy Jackson and Forman their opportunity to see these plays in their original productions, but our own theatrical experience is not really all that different: to satisfy us, a good production must have eloquent speaking of the verse and persuasive choreography of the action. The two aspects of theater are always with us.

Indeed, another "contemporary," the character Macbeth, offered us the same division in an ironic form through his characterization of life as a poor player who does two basic things in his hour on the stage: he struts and he frets. Let us make it a pair of eyewitnesses and a pair of characters, then, by looking more closely at the speech on acting that furnished the title for this study. Hamlet's exact words are worth recalling here:

> Speak the speech, I pray you, as I pronounced it to you, trippingly on the tongue; but if you mouth it as many of your players do, I had as lief the town-crier spoke my lines. Nor do not saw the air too much with your hand, thus, but use all gently; for in the very torrent, tempest, and, as I may say, whirlwind of your passion, you must acquire and beget a temperance that may give it smoothness. . . .
>
> Be not too tame, neither, but let your own discretion be your tutor. Suit the action to the word, the word to the action, with this special observance, that you o'erstep not the modesty of nature. For anything so o'erdone is from the purpose of playing, whose end, both at the first and now, was and is to hold as 'twere the mirror up to nature; to show virtue her feature, scorn her own image, and the very age and body of the time his form and pressure. Now this overdone or come tardy off, though it makes the unskillful laugh, cannot but make the judicious grieve, the censure of the which one must in your allowance o'erweigh a whole theatre of others. O, there be players that I have seen

play—and heard others praise, and that highly—not to speak it profanely, that having neither th'accent of Christians, nor the gait of Christian, pagan, nor man, have so strutted and bellowed that I have thought some of Nature's journeymen had made men, and not made them well, they imitated humanity so abominably. [3.2.1–8, 16–35]

The aesthetic articulated so memorably here is self-demonstrating, not only in the way the actor playing Hamlet presumably exemplifies natural speech and movement as he describes "the art of playing," sawing the air with his hand to demonstrate excessive gesture and then using natural gesture elsewhere, and speaking both clearly and naturally, but also in the constant balancings of the syntax and diction, where speaking and moving are contrasted by means of such terms as word and action, tongue and hand, dumb shows and noise, accent and gait, bellowed and strutted. Not only that: other pairings—"at the first and now," "age and body of the time," "form and pressure," "unskillful" and "judicious," "overdone" and "come tardy off"—testify to the idea that good art, which is also nature, is compounded of different possibilities held in a mutual tension, a kind of ecosystem that balances elements and holds excess in check.

Perhaps the most interesting of Hamlet's pairings is "acquire and beget." The notion that good acting borrows temperance and then creates more of it suggests that art is both mimetic and expressive, imitative and inventive. Its relation to its subject matter is interactive, a process of give-and-take. If it is a mirror, it is a purposive one, held up to nature with revelatory intention: to shame scorn, to encourage virtue, to portray whole eras in their essential form. The give-and-take helps guarantee the "temperance that may give it smoothness" even in representing rough passions. Journeymen actors and journeymen makers, along with injudicious audiences, might find excess—overdoing Termagant, overstepping the modesty of nature, out-Heroding Herod—an exciting prospect. Hamlet knows better and so does his maker. Embedded in Shakespeare's most playful tragedy is a clear articulation of the aesthetic values that drive and shape his art and that characterized, if we are to believe the testimony of his contemporaries, his own personality.

That is why this book could not have a title like *Radical Tragedy*—and I say that without disrespect to the book of that name by Jonathan Dollimore. It is not that the tragedies are not radical; in their experimentation and their willingness to raise large and difficult questions about human nature and Jacobean society, they may well be termed radical. But my consideration has been of the secret of their artistic success, the temperance that gives them smoothness, the balancing of tensions that allows them their scope and intensity, their eloquence and energy. That emphasis has drawn me to demonstrate how Shakespeare achieves harmony by checking excessive stress on any one element or character or possibility, how action and word go different ways but are in the end reunited in a way that no contemporary of this playwright was ever able to equal.

Of course it would be easy to overdo an emphasis on sweet Mr. Shakespeare and his honeyed harmonies. We are talking about tragedy, and tragedy is agonic in nature. Its tensions are painful and racking. It shows a world and a hero in conflict, and its drawing out of that conflict depends on its successful exploitation of tension and struggle. Both speech and action must reflect the struggle, and they may exemplify it too, both within themselves and in their interaction. Thus there is in *Hamlet* the urge to get on with the bloody business of revenge and the impulse to dawdle, to embroider, to pursue analogies and metaphors and curious considerations as one might pursue butterflies in a meadow on a sunny day instead of inside a rotten state or among the strewn bones and flung dirt of an overcrowded graveyard. And thus there is in *Othello* an eloquent hero and a villain who gets around behind the eloquence to mock it and fill our ears with the same kind of poison he uses on his victims in Venice and Cyprus. And thus there is in *Lear* a kind of Chekhovian copresence of fate, history, and agonized reappraisal of the human relation to nature on the one hand and a series of family squabbles, pratfalls, grubby insanity, and sexual obsession on the other. And thus there is in *Macbeth* a mindless, atavistic butchery and low-grade tyranny carried out by a hero so sensitive and poetical that we can often only listen to him in wonder. These wonderful contradictions, so often embodied in apparently disparate stylistic and structural commitments, are Shakespeare's way, it would appear, of responding to tragedy's agonic nature on the one hand and his own divided nature as poet and playwright on the other. If the final result can be recognized as a temperance that gives things smoothness, it must also be acknowledged as a bewildering complexity that makes the plays difficult to produce, to interpret, and to take in as artistic wholes.

It isn't particularly fashionable to talk about artistic wholes these days. We are supposed to be concentrating on the forces that jeopardize the work of art and the artist, that undermine authority and cast doubt on the claims of great art to transcend the circumstances of its own creation. No doubt such forces exist, and play a large part in limiting artistic accomplishment than we used to admit. It is good to let the pendulum swing back from excessive claims about the independence and unity of art, about what artists can accomplish and works of art can mean. In the process there has been, as Guildenstern said of the war of the theaters, "much throwing about of brains." But surely if there were ever works of art that testified to their own success by the regard they have acquired over time, these works are Shakespeare's major tragedies. Even when we discount the cresting tides of Bardolatry and our need for a culture hero and for cultural landmarks like *Hamlet,* we still have something before us that teases us by its very excellence into a consideration of how that excellence functions and of what it may finally consist.

A retrospective consideration of the tragedies from the vantage point afforded by this study leads me to remark on several features that they share. One is the stunningly detailed representation of the hero's mind. Different as they are, Hamlet and Othello and Lear and Macbeth are real and unforgettable to us because we follow, in such a precise and detailed way, the stages of error, suffering, and recognition they undergo between the opening and the close of their dramas. Feeling and knowledge, which are sometimes separated or even opposed in our representations of the human psyche, are not separable in their cases. To be Hamlet is to *know* certain things and at the same time to *feel* their meaning, visited upon the spirit, usually in the form of pain. And so with Othello, Lear, and Macbeth. Each must learn how his own actions lead to new self-knowledge while also creating new pain and suffering, both for himself and for those around him. And to read or see the tragedies is to take this journey of knowledge and feeling with each of the tragic heroes, sharing their agonies and discoveries.

You cannot portray mental events in a drama through action alone. Language is the necessary means by which we are enabled to share the process of self-discovery and personal torment. Each tragic hero must deliberate, often alone and usually at some length, on the meaning of what is happening. And that deliberation, articulated in language, must be in some sense opposed to and juxtaposed against the play's events, its actions. We could say that the hero's actions constitute a close yet separable process running parallel to his thoughts and feelings. The action line interacts with the mental and emotional line but it is also distinct, at times apparently unrelated or even sharply opposed. This opposition sometimes takes the form of a mind–body split, as the following, rather disparate examples suggest:

> It is not, nor it cannot come to good.
> But break my heart, for I must hold my tongue.
>
> > [*H,* 1.2.158–59]

> Was it Hamlet wrong'd Laertes? Never Hamlet.
> If Hamlet from himself be ta'en away,
> And when he's not himself does wrong Laertes,
> Then Hamlet does it not, Hamlet denies it.
>
> > [*H,* 5.2.229–32]

> O, hardness to dissemble!
>
> > [*O,* 3.4.30]

Will you, I pray, demand that demi-devil
Why he hath thus ensnar'd my soul and body?

[*O,* 5.2.302–03]

O Lear, Lear, Lear!
Beat at this gate, that let thy folly in,
And thy dear judgement out!

[*L,* 1.4.279–80]

O! how this mother swells up toward my heart;
Hysterica passio! down, thou climbing sorrow!
Thy element's below. Where is this daughter?

[*L, 2.4.56–58*]

There's no art
To find the mind's construction in the face:
He was a gentleman on whom I built
An absolute trust.

[*M,* 1.4.11–14]

Your face, my Thane, is as a book, where men
May read strange matters. To beguile the time,
Look like the time.

[*M,* 1.5.61–63]

The hero's self-divisions, crucial to his error, to his knowledge, and
to his suffering, are often expressed as divisions between speaking
and acting—thinking or saying one thing and doing another, sometimes deliberately, sometimes helplessly. The process is not exclu-
sive to the tragedies, or indeed to Shakespeare, but it is enacted and
explored in these four plays with a richness and confidence that are
simply breathtaking.

To read them, as I have here, in what we take to be their chro-
nological sequence, is also to witness a portion of Shakespeare's
artistic progress that is singular and fascinating. Artistic development is another slightly taboo topic these days. It is said to be a
kind of illusion foisted on us by excessive claims about the unity

of art and the authority of the artist. But to take Shakespeare at mid-career, working at full stride and at the zenith of his powers in a major genre that he is both recreating and redefining, is to encounter issues of development that can scarcely be overlooked. Current doubts about the phenomenon of development have probably been provoked by simplistic equatings of development with progress or improvement. Certainly, in this case, it is clear that each subsequent play is not necessarily an improvement on the last. *Hamlet* may still remain the favorite when all is said and done. But Shakespeare would have had to be four different people—a variation on his identity that has yet to be proposed, so far as I know—not to have reacted to his own practice as he set about the task of moving on from one try at the tragic mode to another one. These reactions, as I suggested in my introduction, testify to his reach and his restlessness.

Take our first two examples: it is the difference in design between *Hamlet* and *Othello* that strikes us most. Having tried a tragedy in which the hero is everything, dominating his play, Shakespeare appears to have wanted to try one in which the hero is in danger of being displaced by a second character, his antagonist. The self-divided hero, with his tremendous range of rhetorical versatility and verbal play, becomes two separate characters, deeply contrasted in their styles and their lives, each a soldier and each married, each darkened in his mind by his troubled and troubling attitudes toward female sexuality. It is a daring leap to have gone from the one play to the other, but in retrospect it is an exhilarating one.

The move from *Othello* to *Lear* involves a different kind of displacement. Now the plots are doubled, and the character paired with the hero, Gloucester, is a concomitant figure rather than an antagonist. In addition, the dramatic world, which was claustrophobic in *Hamlet* and broader in *Othello,* now opens out into the most capacious dramatic design of which a tragedy might be thought capable. The movements of the two plots, advancing on parallel tracks that sometimes cross or join, involve a substantial cast of characters, and many short scenes are required to facilitate plot business. Shakespeare would return to this geopolitical and quasi-pastoral tragic design in *Antony and Cleopatra,* taking it even further in some ways. It appears to be in part an outgrowth of his interest in the chronicle play, although the specific debt to the double plot of comedy is unmistakable in *King Lear.* A revenge tragedy, followed by a domestic tragedy, followed by a new kind of tragedy that borrowed from three other genres. What would this playwright decide to do next?

He would return, *Macbeth* shows us, to something like the first pattern, the *Hamlet* design, a hero at odds with his world and with an urge to dominate or engulf it. He would retain elements of the domestic tragedy and the geopolitical tragedy, and he would conceive a tragic hero so different that it would occur to few to compare them. The tragic heroes, it might be argued, become increasingly less sympathetic as Shakespeare progresses through his investigation of the genre. Hamlet seems the one most victimized by circumstances, while Othello, Lear, and Macbeth increasingly suggest a pattern of provoking and finally embodying the evil and suffering in their worlds. Even in *Macbeth* the presence of evil is partly externalized in the witches and in Lady Macbeth, but the fact remains that in terms of our sympathy and admiration Macbeth is something like a photographic negative of his earlier counterpart, Hamlet. If the wheel has come full circle, it now has a very different look to it.

The progression is equally interesting on the stylistic front. Having tried such an expansive and dilatory style in *Hamlet,* Shakespeare then refined the dilatory into two types of possibility for *Othello*—the hero's eloquence, particularly exemplified by his power as a storyteller, and the villain's confiding countereloquence, continually subverting the expressive power of language by substituting its deceptive capabilities and by interposing them between us and the honest characters, those who mean what they say. Eloquence becomes a dubious coin of the realm, and a more modern view of language emerges, one that sees it mainly as an instrument of deception and manipulation.

In *King Lear* eloquence becomes so alienated from the world around it that it finally aligns itself with madness, and thus with a social and psychological self-division that turns a whole set of values upside down, questioning established order and the comforting microcosm-macrocosm matchups of traditional philosophy and theology. Now the tragic king's rant, the moldy vein of Herod and Cambyses and even Tamburlaine, is renewed by means of a psychological intimacy: the king is not a distanced figure of fear or fun, but a human being like ourselves, a pained and bewildered spirit. Language undergoes a crisis of expression in *Othello* and *Lear,* but it emerges triumphant, both as a human value and as a dramatic and theatrical instrument.

By the time we reach *Macbeth,* in fact, language has become so powerful that it has taken on magical dimensions of the kind it may have been thought to have only in less sophisticated cultures. Now words may be used not only to entertain, to comfort, to interpret and to deceive, but also to enact desires and create magical events. The range of eloquence, from the emphatic and almost childish chants and rhymes of the witches to the complex and convoluted speeches of the hero and heroine, is as great, in its own way, as it was in the enchanting and bewildering verbal world of *Hamlet.* But we have a distance from it, a detachment about it, that the earlier play never allowed us.

What may impress us most about the power of style in these four plays is the disparate forms it takes, but the progression, each time raising the stakes a little and binding problematic language a little more closely to problematic action, has a fascination all its own. And the progression leads, for better or for worse, to a more critical attitude toward genre.

I have said that Hamlet and Macbeth are similar heroes in some ways, so that their plays, as first and last in this sequence, can be likened to the closing of a circle. I have also suggested that they are as different as a photograph and its negative. The length of the one becomes the brevity of the other, and the jeopardizing of dramatic unity becomes its emphatic reaffirmation. That reaffirmation comes, as I remarked earlier, at some cost; it ushers in a more detached handling of tragedy, a kind of "metageneric" phase, in which Shakespeare will treat not only tragedy, but also comedy and romance, from a perspective that invites us to be as conscious of their limitations as their strengths. That is one reason why *Macbeth* cannot be called Shakespeare's greatest tragedy; it poses too many questions about the genre of which it is such a thoughtful representative. But the metageneric element is matter for another study; the circle I just tried to close is showing signs of opening itself again and the time has come for a brisk—but dignified—exit.

Notes

INTRODUCTION

1 It is, of course, a good deal more successful there than in some of the other plays of the period. For a good defense of Kyd's relative achievement in integrating rhetoric and dramatic action, see Jonas A. Barish, "*The Spanish Tragedy*; or, The Pleasures and Perils of Rhetoric," in *Elizabethan Theatre,* ed. John Russell Brown and Bernard Harris, Stratford-upon-Avon Studies 9 (London, 1966), pp. 59–85.

1. LARGE DISCOURSE AND THRIFTY ACTION IN *HAMLET*

1 Francis Berry, *The Shakespearean Inset* (New York, 1965). Berry calls insets "a break from the dramatic *now,* a shift of tense accompanied by a vocal change . . . to suit that shift" (p. 11). He distinguishes five types of inset: Expository; Required by Interior Plot; Voluntary (for instance, Mercutio's "Queen Mab" speech); Song; Play-within-a-play (p. 12). Of *Hamlet* he comments, "It is not surprising that this play is compact of Insets, salient or recessive, and that these Insets connect with each other—salient with salient, recessive with recessive—either in front of, or in the background of, the dominant surface plane presented to listeners *and* spectators" (p. 117).

2 Bert O. States, "The Word-pictures in *Hamlet,*" *Hudson Review* 26, no. 3, (Autumn 1973): 510–22. The quotation is from pages 510–11. States has been round the *Hamlet* territory in a very nimble fashion, and I

shall be crossing his tracks at a number of points. He is the glass of fashion and the mold of form for anyone who wants to consider the lively, garrulous style of this play.

3 For a discussion of dilation in terms of its use in *Othello,* particularly in the phrase "close dilations," see Patricia Parker, "Shakespeare and Rhetoric: 'Dilation' and 'Delation' in *Othello,*" in *Shakespeare and the Question of Theory,* ed. Patricia Parker and Geoffrey Hartman (London, 1985), pp. 54–74. She clearly demonstrates the dual meaning of *dilate* as "to amplify" (especially in rhetoric) and "to delay." She makes a less convincing case for the related meaning of "to accuse" (*delate*) within her interpretation of *Othello.*

4 Citations from the play are drawn from the Arden edition of *Hamlet,* ed. Harold Jenkins (London and New York, 1982).

5 David Young, "*Hamlet,* Son of *Hamlet,*" in *Perspectives on Hamlet,* ed. William G. Holzberger and Peter B. Waldeck (Lewisberg, Pa., 1973), pp. 184–206. See especially, pp. 195–96.

6 States, "Word-pictures," p. 511.

7 *Holy Sonnets, I,* from Charles M. Coffin, ed., *The Complete Poetry and Selected Prose of John Donne* (Modern Library, 1952), p. 247.

8 My own view tends toward the notion that Marston was responding to the popularity of Shakespeare's revival of the genre and of Kyd's old play, although the final text of *Hamlet,* especially the passage about the child players, would seem to postdate Marston's play. The issues and evidences are well summarized in Jenkins's Arden edition, pages 7–13.

9 Jonson's attacks on the genre were frequent, but I have especially in mind the Induction to *Bartholomew Fair* (1614): "He that will swear Jeronimo and Andronicus are the best plays yet, shall pass unexpected at here as a man whose judgement shows it is constant, and hath stood still these five and twenty, or thirty years."

10 Again, Jenkins's summary is useful. See Jenkins, ed., *Hamlet,* pp. 97–101.

11 Young, "*Hamlet,* Son of *Hamlet,*" pp. 190–94.

12 David Young, "Where the Bee Sucks: A Triangular Study of *Doctor Faustus, The Alchemist,* and *The Tempest,*" in *Shakespeare's Romances Reconsidered,* ed. Carol McGinnis and Henry E. Jacobs (Lincoln, Neb., 1978), pp. 149–66.

13 See, especially, James L. Calderwood, *To Be and Not to Be: Negation and Metadrama in 'Hamlet'* (New York, 1983).

14 The argument for this staging is pursued in John Doebler, *Shakespeare's Speaking Pictures: Studies in Iconic Imagery* (Albuquerque, N.M., 1974).

15 The argument for the ghost's location under the stage as indicative of his diabolic origin is fully pursued (perhaps too fully) in Nevill Coghill, *Shakespeare's Professional Skills* (Cambridge, 1965), pp. 10–13.

16 Donne's poem "The Relic" begins, "When my grave is broke up againe / Some second guest to entertaine," and Shakespeare's epitaph is aimed at preventing just that contingency. Since the other familiar instance of broken graves was the imaginative picture people carried around of the Second Coming and the Day of Judgment, the disturbing of old bones to make way for fresh corpses must have seemed a bitterly ironic version of the doctrine of corporeal resurrection.

2. STORYTELLING AND COMPLICITY IN *OTHELLO*

1 Other accounts of the play have remarked on the importance of Othello's storytelling powers. Ross McDonald, "Othello, Thorello, and the Problem of the Foolish Hero," *Shakespeare Quarterly* 30, no. 1 (1979), describes Othello's "histrionic talent" and adds, "As he recounts how he wooed Desdemona by telling the story of his life, Othello manages to graft upon the tender story of their courtship an abstract of the thrilling tale that won her" (p. 61). Marjorie Pryse, in "Lust for Audience: An Interpretation of *Othello*," *ELH* 43, no. 4 (1976), notes that "If Othello wins Desdemona because he is a good storyteller, however, he loves her because she is such a flattering audience" (p. 463). Pryse's essay, unfortunately, deals mainly in dubious sexual innuendoes; for instance, Othello's mention of men whose heads do grow beneath their shoulders is an attempt "to appropriate the phallic powers of young men" (p. 463). His narratives are for Pryse a cover-up for his impotence, and his tendency to conduct his courtship by telling stories may have "masked his inability to woo her in any other way" (p. 465). Stephen Greenblatt, *Renaissance Self-Fashioning* (Chicago, 1980), offers a persuasive account of Iago's "ceaseless narrative invention" (p. 235) and the "submission to narrativity" (p. 237) that is characteristic of everyone in the play. See also the article by Patricia Parker, "Shake-

speare and Rhetoric: 'Dilation' and 'Delation' in *Othello,*" cited in note 3 to my *Hamlet* chapter.

2 As I indicated in my Introduction, I am quoting from the text of M. R. Ridley's Arden edition of *Othello* (London, 1958). Ridley's sometimes eccentric preferences for Quarto over Folio readings are already evident in this first citation from the play: "set phrase of peace" rather than "soft phrase of peace," and "proceedings am I" versus "proceeding I am." I prefer the music of "soft phrase" over the less interesting "set phrase," but rather than quarrel with Ridley in further examples I will silently accept his text and leave questions of preference to my readers. I think, in fact, that many of Ridley's changes in the traditional, Folio-based text of Othello are illuminating as well as thought-provoking, but that is matter for a different discussion.

3 In his fondness for the narrative that turns into drama by means of the materialization of the story's characters on the stage, Shakespeare may have been recalling a device first used by George Peele in *The Old Wives' Tale.* Old Madge begins her story by the fireside for her visitors, but its "telling" becomes the play upon the entrance of the actors who will perform it. A similar transition is effected as we move from induction to play proper in *The Taming of the Shrew.*

4 G. K. Hunter, "Othello and Colour Prejudice," in *Dramatic Identities and Cultural Tradition* (New York, 1978), argues, "The imposition of Iago's vulgar prejudices on Othello ('These Moors are changeable in their wills,' etc.) is so successful that it takes over not only Othello but almost all the critics. But Iago's suppression of Othello into the vulgar prejudice about him can only be sustained as the truth if we ignore the end of the play. The wonderful recovery here of the sense of ethical meaning in the world, even in the ashes of all that embodied meaning— this requires that we see the final speech of Othello as more than that of a repentant blackamoor 'cheering himself up,' as Mr. Eliot phrased it. It is in fact a marvelous *stretto* of all the themes that have sounded throughout the play. Othello is the 'base Indian' who threw away the white pearl Desdemona, but he is also the state servant and Christian who, when the Infidel or 'black Pagan' within him seemed to triumph, 'Took by the throat the circumcised dog / And smote him thus'" (pp. 56–57).

5 A. C. Bradley, in *Shakespearean Tragedy* (Cleveland, 1955), calls it "of all of Shakespeare's tragedies ... the most painfully exciting and the

most terrible" (p. 145). Marvin Rosenberg, in *The Masks of Othello* (California, 1961), traces the history of compassionate response the play has evoked. The earliest such reaction comes from a letter written in 1610 by Henry Jackson, a student at Oxford, to a friend. It reads in part (translated from the Latin) as follows: "In the last few days the King's players have been here. They acted with enormous applause to full houses.... And they had tragedies which they acted decorously and appropriately. In which not only the speeches but also the actions moved some to tears. Indeed Desdemona, killed in our midst by her husband, though she argued her case for the best, moved us even more when dead; while lying in bed she called forth pity by her very countenance" (see Geoffrey Tillotson, "*Othello* and *The Alchemist* at Oxford in 1610," *TLS* [July 20, 1933]: 494).

6 Edward Bullough, "Psychical Distance as a Factor in Art and an Aesthetic Principle," *British Journal of Psychology* 5 (1912): 87–98.

7 A number of them have noted the general importance of Iago's extensive confiding in the audience. Marvin Spevack, in *Shakespeare and the Allegory of Evil* (New York, 1958), notes that Iago is "outside the play" insofar as "he is the showman who produces it and the chorus who interprets it, and his essential relationship is with the audience" (p. 31). Bertrand Evans, in *Shakespeare's Tragic Practice* (Oxford, 1979), observes that through most of the play "we share our awareness with none but Iago" (p. 116). In *Othello as Tragedy: Some Problems of Judgment and Feeling* (Cambridge, 1980), Jane Adamson argues that "Iago's disclosures leave us as mere onlookers, with no option but to remain silent with him as if in enforced complicity, excruciatingly bound to him by the knowledge we cannot share with those who (if we only could speak) might avert the disaster which will otherwise befall them. This is surely one reason why *Othello* is so continuously painful" (p. 66).

8 See especially Alvin Kernan's Introduction to the Signet edition (Sylvan Barnet, general editor) of the play (New York, 1963).

9 Bradley, *Shakespearean Tragedy,* p. 172.

3. THE MAPS OF *KING LEAR*

1 David Young, *The Heart's Forest: A Study of Shakespeare's Pastoral Plays* (New Haven and London, 1972). See also Maynard Mack, *King Lear in Our Time* (Berkeley, 1965), esp. pp. 63–66.

2 Susan Snyder, in *The Comic Matrix of Shakespeare's Tragedies* (Princeton, 1979), gives a useful survey of the comic elements in *Lear*.

3 The king–beggar pairing had made frequent verbal appearances in Shakespeare's plays, from the line in *Love's Labour's Lost*: "Is there not a ballad, boy, of the King and the Beggar?" through *Twelfth Night*'s "Thou mayst say, the king lies by a beggar, if a beggar dwell near him"; *Hamlet*'s "a king may go a progress through the guts of a beggar"; and in *All's Well That Ends Well*: "The king's a beggar, now the play is done." Given Shakespeare's apparent interest and the suggestion of wide currency we get from these frequent alignments of the apex and nadir of the social order, it was only a matter of time, one feels, before they found themselves on stage as paired characters. Ripeness is all.

4 Jack Murrah, a student of mine at the Breadloaf School of English in the summer of 1983, wrote a paper on the geography of *King Lear* that helped shape my own thinking about the importance of the play's maps, literal and metaphorical.

5 The sources and meanings in this passage are summarized in the New Variorum edition of the play, edited by H. H. Furness (Philadelphia, 1880), pp. 205–06.

6 The unique use of perspective in Edgar's description of the cliff is discussed by Marshall McLuhan in *The Gutenberg Galaxy* (Toronto, 1962): "Shakespeare seems to have missed due recognition for having in *King Lear* made the first, and so far as I know, the only piece of verbal three-dimensional perspective in any literature" (p. 15).

4. PRIMITIVISM AND SOPHISTICATION IN *MACBETH*

1 As quoted in the Introduction to Kenneth Muir's Arden edition (9th ed.; London, 1962), p. xiv.

2 Alfred Harbage, *William Shakespeare: A Reader's Guide* (New York, 1963), p. 379.

3 For a useful discussion of the relation between regicide and the possible origins of tragedy in rituals of sacrifice and succession, see John Holloway, *The Story of the Night* (London, 1961), especially chapter 8, and Maynard Mack, Jr., *Killing the King* (New Haven, 1973). Harry Berger, in "The Early Scenes of *Macbeth*: Preface to a New Interpretation,"

ELH 47, no. 1 (Spring 1980), notes that Holloway's archetypal reading discovers a "deep structure informing the surface action" (p. 2).

4 Roman Polanski's film of the play, while very uneven in quality, picked up the washing motif effectively by having Lady Macduff in the midst of bathing her son when the assassins arrived. It seemed almost as if Polanski had discovered a lost stage direction.

5 These references are explored by Cleanth Brooks in his famous essay "The Naked Babe and the Cloak of Manliness," in Cleanth Brooks, *The Well Wrought Urn* (New York, 1947).

6 This issue is usefully discussed in Michael Goldman, *Acting and Action in Shakespearean Tragedy* (Princeton, 1985), Introduction.

7 David Young, *The Heart's Forest* (New Haven, 1972), p. 117.

8 A. P. Rossiter, in *Angel With Horns* (London, 1961), speaks of "Macbeth's *impulsion* . . . to assert *his* pattern on the world: to make Macbeth Scotland. Instead he finds he has made Scotland Macbeth: his damned soul has infected a whole country, even the whole universe" (p. 211).

9 Cleanth Brooks's essay again comes first to mind.

10 John Kadyk, paper written at the Breadloaf School of English, summer 1983.

11 For this and subsequent information about word frequency in the play I am indebted to *Macbeth: A Concordance to the Text of the First Folio,* ed. T. H. Howard-Hill, Oxford Shakespeare Concordances (Oxford: Clarendon Press, 1971).

Index

Adamson, Jane, 147*n*
Arden of Feversham (author unknown), 104
Art: as compounded of tensions, 133–34; issue of wholeness in, 135
Aside, convention of, 63–64

Beckett, Samuel, 43
Berger, Harry, 148*n*
Berry, Francis, 10, 143*n*
Bevington, David, xi
Bradley, A. C., 74, 146*n*, 147*n*
Brooks, Cleanth, 149*n*
Bullough, Edward, 147*n*

Calderwood, James L., 145*n*
Coghill, Nevill, 145*n*

Dilation: choice of as term, 10–11; four directions of in *Hamlet,* 13–14; directions mingling in *Hamlet* soliloquies, 17–18;

awareness of in *Hamlet* characters, 20–21; and subdilation, 21–22; at close of *Hamlet,* 29–30
Dilations: effect of contrast in, 11–12; among Polonius's family, 12
Doebler, John, 145*n*
Dollimore, Jonathan, 134
Donne, John: Holy Sonnet I, 28; on reuse of graves, 42, 145*n*

Eliot, T. S.: objections to *Othello* by, 46, 58, 59
Evans, Bertrand, 147*n*

Forman, Simon, 99–100, 116, 131–32
Freud, Sigmund, 107
Furness, H. H., x, 148*n*

Giraudoux, Jean, 6
Goldman, Michael, 149*n*

151